WALKING
—THE—
FOREST BOUNDS
OF DARTMOOR

MICHAEL HEDGES

Peninsula
Press

First published in 2004 by Peninsula Press,
an imprint of Forest Publishing
Woodstock
Liverton
Newton Abbot
Devon TQ12 6JJ

British Library Cataloguing in Publication Data

A catalogue record for this book is available from the British Library.

ISBN 1–872640–53–2

Editorial, design and layout by:
Mike Lang

Front cover illustration by:
John W. Taylor

Typeset by:
Carnaby Typesetting, Torquay, Devon TQ1 1EG

Printed and bound in Great Britain by:
Cromwell Press Ltd, Trowbridge, Wiltshire BA14 0XB

Contents

Acknowledgements

I should like to thank my publisher, Mike Lang, for producing this, my third book, and for his ever-attentive editor's eye!
I am also grateful to Len Jones and Bill Radcliffe for providing me with references and photocopies of old papers relating to the Forest of Dartmoor.

Introduction

The Forest of Dartmoor was established more than 750 years ago yet, despite its origins in the mists of time, today it continues to have a significant influence on the everyday lives of the people of Dartmoor. Almost everything that lies within its modern boundary is owned by the Duchy of Cornwall, that is the estates and lands belonging to the Duke of Cornwall - a title bestowed traditionally upon the male heir to the British throne. Many people and businesses located in the central basin of Dartmoor are therefore, at the time of writing, tenants of HRH Prince Charles.

The land occupied by the Forest includes the remotest and wildest parts of Dartmoor. As long ago as 1240, by writ of Henry III, twelve jurors rode around the outside of a central area of Dartmoor to fix the boundary of what had been a royal hunting ground, or forest, so that the king could then hand the land over to his brother Richard, the Earl of Poitou and Cornwall. This fixing of the boundary was the first known *perambulation* of the Forest of Dartmoor. The jurors recorded the points and features along the boundary in a document, a copy of which still exists to this day. In 1608 a further perambulation (presented to a Survey Court in 1609) was carried out; the new boundary included many of the locations recorded in 1240, but some intermediate bounds were added. Since then there has been much argument about the precise location of some of the places named in both perambulations, and today the modern boundary recognised by the Duchy varies in its detail from both of these early attempts to fix the bounds.

The story of the boundary of the Forest of Dartmoor is full of fascination. That so remote an area of moorland should have been the subject of such detailed examination is astonishing, until one considers how important it was to establish the extent of the rights of land use of both the common people and what was to become the Duchy. More mundane matters come to mind; did the original jurors of 1240 have much previous knowledge of Dartmoor, were they assisted by local people, why were certain points chosen? I shall speculate on the answers to some of these questions in the course of this book.

Most attractive of all about the Forest of Dartmoor is the landscape that it encompasses. The 1240 boundary is just over 43 miles in circumference and within it is some of the most remote upland in England, where many of the rivers of Devon have their sources. There is also a miraculously large number of surviving archaeological relics, ranging from 'prehistoric' sites to those of early 20th century industry. For anyone wishing to escape from the pressures of the modern world for a few hours, there are few better ways than to spend a fine, dry day walking within or around the Forest of Dartmoor.

This book is a guide to walking the circumference of the 1240 Forest boundary, based on my personal experiences. I did not walk the whole perimeter in one stretch; instead, I preferred to tackle it in a more relaxed manner so as to appreciate better the variety of the landscape and the outstanding features, and walked it over a period from March 2000 to March 2002 in twelve stages, starting and finishing on Cosdon Hill.

If you are tempted to follow in my footsteps and are not familiar with high Dartmoor, there are a number of precautions you must take before setting out and I have summarised these below.

Military Activity: The primary risk to a walker on northern Dartmoor is the regular live firing that takes place in the Okehampton, Willsworthy and Merrivale ranges. These are used by many branches of the armed forces and information on firing times can be obtained by telephoning the free phone number 0800 458 4868 or by visiting the website www.dartmoor-ranges.co.uk. On firing days, red flags are flown from prominent points on the range boundaries and lookouts are posted to watch for stray walkers. The boundaries of the three ranges are marked on the ground with prominent red and white marker posts bearing warning signs. Notices of firing times are posted in pubs and other public buildings, such as the High Moorland Visitor Centre in Princetown.

Obviously, when live firing is in progress, you should keep well away from the ranges. When walking on the moor, unfamiliar metal objects should not be touched, as they could be unexploded mortars, but should be reported to the police or the military. There have been instances of serious injury caused by people picking up such objects, some of which have been of World War II vintage. That said, the range authorities have strived to clear the moor of unexploded ordnance, but there is always a risk that more will turn up. Sometimes cartridge cases from expended blanks are left on the ground and occasionally these can include undetonated rounds, so again these should not be touched.

There is no live firing on the southern high moor, but 'dry' firing (ie with blanks) is sometimes carried out there and the same precautions mentioned above should be observed.

Adequate Clothing and Equipment: This subject might almost merit a book in itself, but I shall be brief and to the point. Above all, I try to walk on Dartmoor when it is not raining and when arctic conditions do not prevail. It is very uncomfortable and no pleasure to walk in pouring rain. If you go out on the high moor alone when there is snow or a very low ambient temperature, then you are running a high risk. If you have an accident that prevents you walking down off the moor, such as twisting an ankle on scree, you will be under serious threat from low temperatures, exposure, hypothermia and worse.

Boots: On days after rain, particularly in winter, wellington boots are often the most practical footwear. In summer, and in drier conditions underfoot, a good pair of walking boots is the best way of avoiding sore feet and blisters. Unfortunately, with boots, 'good' usually means expensive - I have a pair (price £99 in 2004) that have cushioned soles and heels and a Gore-Tex lining. Provided I tie the laces tight enough (but obviously not too tight) so that my feet do not slip around inside the boots, they are superb for long-distance moorland walking: my feet stay dry even if I continually sink two or three inches into wet ground as I walk, and on hard ground the cushioned soles and heels prevent blisters from forming.

There are also trainer-type boots available; most of these lack any waterproofing, but they do give good ankle support, which is essential for rough walking.

Trousers: I always carry a pair of waterproof leggings in my backpack, apart from on warm summer days. Then I don't bother and just wear a light pair of cotton or linen trousers. Shorts should never be worn because of the risk of sheep tics embedding themselves in the soft flesh of walkers' legs!

On the milder days of spring or autumn I wear the same type of lighter trousers, but in cold weather I wear denim jeans.

Coat: On warm summer days I walk in a tee shirt, but have a fleece, or thin cagoule, in my backpack just in case the weather changes unexpectedly. Otherwise I walk in a waterproof jacket (I haven't splashed out on a Gore-Tex lined coat though) with a detachable internal fleece. If conditions become rather sweaty, the waterproof outside portion is thin enough to be rolled up and carried inside my backpack and I walk in the fleece.

Other clothing: A good pair of gloves is essential on a colder day, although often the exertion of walking means they can be removed after the first mile. I have a flat cap, a baseball cap and a woolly hat which I select according to the time of year. The baseball cap is very good at keeping a strong summer sun out of the eyes and for protecting the baldies, or near-baldies (that's me!), from sunstroke. Otherwise, in cold weather, my flat cap prevents heat loss and I find I can use it to control body temperature to some degree. When I walk in a northerly or easterly wind in winter, my woolly hat offers ear protection. A scarf makes walking much more bearable in a biting wind.

Equipment: I always carry a backpack, in my case one of 35-litre capacity with a (partially) waterproof exterior with side pockets. It contains more than enough food and drink for the walk, a 1:25,000 scale map of Dartmoor, a compass, penknife, spare bootlaces, a referee's whistle (for attracting attention if I should be in difficulties), as well as the appropriate items of clothing mentioned above. All these are essential items which should always be carried.

I now also carry a mobile phone with me. While this might be thought intrusive, there is always an 'off' button to prevent my communion with the landscape from being interrupted! But more positively, it might be a boon if I were to break or twist an ankle in a remote part of the moor. In a Dartmoor valley there will often be no signal, but on higher ground there is quite often a good reception, especially if your particular network company has cells mounted on the North Hessary Tor TV mast.

Other precautions: If I am walking alone on the moor I always leave a note of my route with my family and try not to deviate far from it. I also try to start my walks at a fairly gentle pace until I have warmed up. I usually find that I get 'a second wind' (nothing to do with my sandwiches!) during a long walk, but that the more unfit I am, the longer it takes before that extra energy comes through.

Finally, a certain degree of fitness is needed for walking on the high moor; the more you walk, the fitter you'll become. But beginners should not tackle a really long walk from the outset unless they are already fit. Moreover, people with certain medical conditions may need to take a doctor's advice before walking long distances on rough ground - it certainly gets the heart pumping away!

Good luck with your Dartmoor walking!

Michael Hedges
November 2004

The Forest of Dartmoor

Before I take the reader around the Forest boundary it is worth pausing to look at the historical origins of the Forest and to consider why it is still significant. In doing this, I shall make a determined effort to avoid repeating the worst errors of the history books inflicted upon me at school during the 1960s. I found, probably in common with many others, that my history textbooks were written in an obtuse manner, using words and expressions that had been lifted straight from old documents without any attempt to explain their meaning and educate the reader - which was, after all, the purpose!

When one comes to read old papers and books about the Forest of Dartmoor the same unfortunate trend is readily apparent in many cases. But, in this chapter, any old or specialised words will be explained, not left hanging in the air.

And the very first of these words is 'forest' itself - what was it? Well, a *forest* was not, as is commonly supposed, a large area of woodland. It was the name given to a royal hunting ground - with or without trees. In the more elegant words of the late 16th century writer Manwood it was 'A certain territory of woody grounds and fruitful pastures, privileged for wild beasts and fowls of forest chase and warren, to rest and abide there in the safe protection of the King, for his delight and pleasure.' In this context 'beasts' were red, fallow and roe deer, along with wild boar, for which the collective term was *venison*.

The concept of a forest is believed to have existed at the time of King Canute (who ruled from 1016 - 1035), but it became of historical prominence with the invasion by the Normans in 1066. Draconian laws protecting the status of a forest already existed on the continent, and in 1079 William the Conqueror imposed them on England, when large parts of the country were *afforested*, that is became subject to forest law. This was separate to common law and had its own courts and court officials.

As well as protecting venison, forest law also protected the *vert*, or green undergrowth, on which venison fed. One effect of this was that the population in a forest could not gather fuel, nor could they enclose forest land for agriculture. The penalties for transgression were severe; death was the penalty for killing venison, while shooting at venison warranted hands being cut off and the fate of anyone caught disturbing venison was to be blinded. No-one was allowed into a forest at night and those responsible for the upkeep of paths were subject to penalties if they neglected their duties, for the simple reason that a traveller who strayed from a path might disturb the venison.

The severity of these laws caused much unrest amongst rich and poor alike. In Devon a petition of protest had some effect, for in 1204, in return for a fine of 10,000 marks being paid by the people of Devon, King John disafforested all of Devon and Cornwall, with the exception of Dartmoor and Exmoor. These areas were retained because, as recorded in the Domesday Book, they belonged to the Crown. Interestingly the Domesday Book is the earliest known document where Dartmoor is equated with Lydford, and for centuries thereafter the parish of Lydford consisted mostly of the Forest of Dartmoor, along with an area around the village itself.

In 1217 a charter of Henry III, the First Charter of the Forest, disafforested much of the rest of England and mitigated the severity of forest law, to the extent that death or mutilation could no longer be imposed as a penalty for breaching it.

The 1217 disafforestation appears to have had little practical effect until a further charter of 1224, under which formal *perambulations*, or definition of boundaries, are thought to have taken place.

In 1239 Henry III granted the Forest of Dartmoor and the manor of Lydford to his brother Richard, the Earl of Poitou and Cornwall. At this point forest law ceased to be applicable within the Forest of Dartmoor and technically the area became a *chase*, that is a hunting ground in private ownership and subject to common law, not forest law. Nonetheless, in this book I shall follow the convention of all other Dartmoor writers and refer to the 'Forest boundary', although more correctly it should be called the 'chase boundary'.

In order to confirm the boundary of the earl's land, or perhaps to review an earlier boundary perambulation (of which there are no records or other evidence), Henry III ordered by a writ dated 13th June 1240 that a perambulation should be carried out by twelve jurors appointed by the Sheriff of Devon. So it was that the boundary that forms the subject of this book was defined, the task being completed on 24th July, just under six weeks after the writ had been served by the king.

The twelve jurors allocated the task of perambulating the bounds of the Forest were:-

William Brewer	Henry, the son of Henry
Guy Breteville	William Trenchard
William Wydeworthy	Philip Parrer
Hugo Bellay	Nicholas Heamton
Richard Gyffard	William Moreleghe
Odo Treverbyn	Durant, the son of Boton

The boundary delineated by these gentlemen in that first perambulation passed through the following points, some of which I have listed in the old language along with the modern place name (which in a number of cases is by no means certain):-

Hoga de Cossdonne (Cosdon Hill)
Parva Hundetorre (Hound Tor)

Thurlestone (Watern Tor)
Wotesbrokelakesfote (Hew Lake Foot)
Heigheston (The Longstone on Shovel Down)
Langestone (The Heath Stone)
Turbary of Alberysheved (possibly Metheral Marsh)
Wallebroke (probably an erroneous repetition of the later reference to the
   Wallabrook)
Furnum Regis (King's Oven)
Wallebrokeshede (head of the Wallabrook)
Along the Wallabrook to its confluence with the East Dart
Dartmeet
Along the River Dart to confluence with the O Brook (Okebrokysfote)
Up the O Brook to Dry Lake tin streamings (la Dryeworke)
Dryfeldford (intersection of the boundary with the Sandy Way)
Battyshull (Ryder's Hill)
Head of the Western Wellabrook
Down the Western Wellabrook to its confluence with the Avon
Ester Whyteburghe (Eastern Whitebarrow)
Red Lake Foot
Grymsgrove (Erme Head)
Elysburghe (Eylesbarrow)
Syward's Cross (Nun's Cross)
Ysfother (South Hessary Tor)
'another Ysfother' (North Hessary Tor)
Mystor (Great Mis Tor)
Mewyburghe (White Barrow)
Lullingesfote (Limsboro Cairn)
Rakernesbrokysfote (Rattlebrook Foot)
Up the Rattlebrook to its head
La Westsolle (Stenga Tor)
Ernestorre (Yes Tor)
Chapel of St Michael de Halgestoke (Cullever Steps, although some place
   it further north, to the east of Lower Halstock)
Hoga de Cossdonne (Cosdon Hill)

(These are the points that I visited in the perambulation I undertook in
stages between March 2000 and March 2002.)

Richard's son, Edmund, succeeded to the title of Earl of Cornwall and, on his
death in 1300, the manor of Lydford and the Forest of Dartmoor reverted to
the Crown. However, on 17th March 1337, Edward III granted these lands to
his son Edward, Prince of Wales, who was also Duke of Cornwall and would
later become known as the Black Prince. The Forest of Dartmoor has
belonged to the Duchy of Cornwall ever since then, and HRH Prince Charles

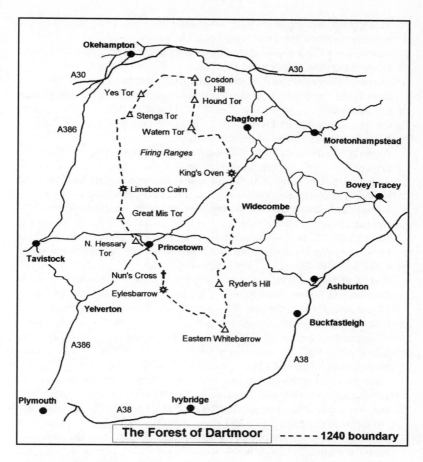

The Forest of Dartmoor ----- 1240 boundary

is the 24th Duke of Cornwall.

In 1608 a further perambulation was carried out and presented to a Survey Court in August 1609. This modified certain parts of the boundary and sought to clarify other bound points. In some cases additional points were added between the bound points established in 1240.

Even today one part of the Forest (now Duchy) boundary is subject to some dispute. This is the section between Erme Head and Eylesbarrow on southern Dartmoor. The Duchy holds that the boundary runs from Erme Head to Plym Steps and then to Eylesbarrow, whereas others maintain, perhaps unsurprisingly, that it encloses less land than this and, in fact, runs from Erme

Head to Plym Head via Broad Rock, then down the Plym to a point 400 yards downstream of Plym Ford and finally to Eylesbarrow.

Nowadays the Duke of Cornwall does not receive any payment from the Civil List (a system of financial grant paid by the government to the senior members of the royal family), but relies solely on the Duchy estates for income. These comprise 141,000 acres of land in 25 counties, including much of the coastline and estuaries of Cornwall, Dartmoor prison, shops, office buildings and even The Oval cricket ground in London, and in 2002/03 generated a surplus of almost £10m.

So the boundary of the Forest has much significance to Dartmoor residents to this day. Nearly all buildings and land on Dartmoor inside the modern line of the boundary (not exactly, but very close to the route I shall be describing in this book) are owned by the Duchy, and their occupants have to pay rent to it. Outside the boundary, land and properties are in the freehold ownership of private organisations and individuals. It is quite rare for the Duchy to sell any of its property! On Dartmoor, the local Duchy office is situated in Princetown, in the building which was formerly the Duchy Hotel and which now also includes the High Moorland Visitor Centre.

It is worthwhile at this stage mentioning the farms known as *ancient tenements*. These were established in the earliest days of afforestation on Dartmoor and their occupants had a form of freehold ownership called copyhold and so did not have to pay any rent. They enjoyed the rights to graze animals, cut peat for fuel and take stone in the Forest. In return they were obliged to attend the Forest Court at Lydford and to assist with the annual *drifts*, or the driving of all grazing animals off parts of the moor.

There were 35 ancient tenements in total. These were at Babeny (3), Broom Park, Dury, Huccaby (5), Prince Hall, Sherberton (3), Bellever (2), Brown Berry, Hartland, Lower Merripit, Riddon, Brimpts (3), Dunnabridge (4), Hexworthy (3), Pizwell (3) and Runnage (2).

Rights of Common are also very significant in respect of the Forest of Dartmoor. Commoners' rights have existed from far back in history, and since disafforestation all residents of Devon, excluding (for some unknown reason) those in Barnstaple and Totnes, have been able to lawfully enjoy commoners' rights on the unenclosed lands of Dartmoor - the Dartmoor Commons. People who occupied land in the parishes abutting the boundary of the Forest also had the rights, in return for a form of rent known as *fines villarum*, to graze animals on the Forest during daylight hours, cut peat for fuel (the right of *turbary*), dig stone and sand to repair their houses and land, and to take heath for thatching and litter. Such people were said to have *venville* rights. These rights could be extended to include night grazing by payment of additional money.

Those who did not hold venville rights could also graze their animals on the Forest, but only on payment of a higher amount than those who did have venville rights.

So the establishment of the Forest (and later Duchy) bounds spawned a range of special rights and obligations that formed dominant influences on the lives of those who sought to make a living on and around Dartmoor.

Now it's time to close the history book and venture out on to the moor itself in the steps of those who first defined the bounds of the Forest of Dartmoor.

One of two 'cobra's head' iron boundary markers carrying the badly-worn inscription 'FB' (Forest Bound), one being at Eylesbarrow and the other here on South Hessary Tor.

1. Cosdon Hill to The Heath Stone – 6.5 miles

Starting point: The car park above Cullever Steps, next to the Black-a-ven Brook.
Grid ref: SX 601 919.
Other important information: Walk lies partly within the Okehampton Firing Range.
Total length of walk: Around 15 miles. One alternative would be to park at Cullever Steps and arrange to be met by car at the Heath Stone and be driven back to the starting point. This would shorten the walk to $8^1/2$ miles.

Cosdon Hill is where the perambulators of 1240 began and finished their work for Henry III. It must have seemed fitting to have selected this brooding whaleback hill for that purpose, as even today, when one is travelling along the A30 from Exeter, Cosdon dominates the prospect of north-eastern Dartmoor. It is also unlike many other hills on Dartmoor; there is no summit rock outcrop or tor and in fact it is very like the round-topped Carnedds in Snowdonia. Indeed, to look northwards from its summit is like looking from the foredeck of a giant ship and there is a distinct feeling of being on the roof

Part of the summit cairn on Cosdon Hill, with High Willhays, Yes Tor and West Mil Tor on the skyline.

of Dartmoor. On a clear day the view extends as far south as Western Whitebarrow, above the Avon valley on southern Dartmoor.

To reach Cosdon Hill from Cullever Steps, head just south of east and follow Irishman's Wall up over the Belstone Tors. Then drop down into the Taw valley, crossing the river at a convenient point, and continue uphill in the

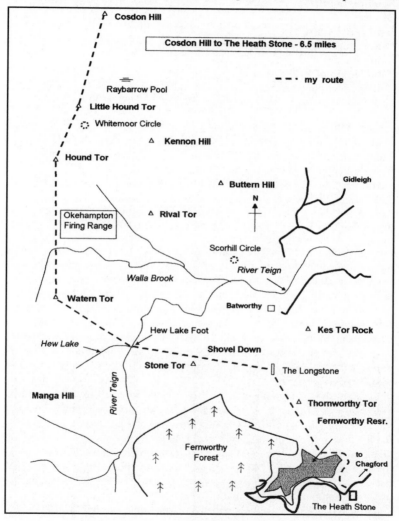

Reproduced by permission of Ordnance Survey on behalf of The Controller of Her Majesty's Stationery Office, © Crown Copyright 100042123.

same direction. At this point you are already on the western slopes of Cosdon, and a long plod, including passing over a shoulder of ground known as Queenie Meads, will eventually bring you to the summit.

After an obligatory pause to rest and take in the momentous stature and status of Cosdon, start your perambulation by heading to the south, where a white ribbon of path undulates away over Little Hound Tor to Hound Tor. Extensive views and the easy walking over the finely-crushed granite of the path make it an exhilarating experience to walk south from Cosdon. The western slopes of Big Whit Hill and Little Hound Tor are cloaked in bracken and, on the other side, the treacherous wet patches of Raybarrow Pool glint menacingly in the long grass. To the south, a lone South Tawton parish boundstone is visible between Little Hound Tor and Kennon Hill.

Further on, heading over Little Hound Tor itself (just a small pile of rocks on what might loosely and flatteringly be called its summit), your eye will be drawn by the great sweeps of brown and green vegetation that descend the slopes to the Small Brook on the valley floor to the west. Eastwards the view extends to Kestor Rock, while further around to the south are Fernworthy Forest and Sittaford Tor, with Whitemoor Stone and Circle a few metres away across the heather.

Continue to Hound Tor, another fairly nondescript, flattish rock stump, but one that gives yet more fine views of northern Dartmoor. Immediately below it, to the south-east, light reflects off the channels of water meandering through Gallaven Mire. The summit rocks of Wild Tor and Watern Tor are now also in view and, to follow the Forest boundary, you should make a beeline for the top of Watern Tor. The short, firm turf underfoot gives an easy walk diagonally down the slope and into the valley of the Wallabrook.

On this valley floor is a large patch of spiky grass that partly conceals the wet ooze of Wild Tor Well. To the right, the scree-studded slope of Wild Tor stretches up into the sky, while ahead looms the northern slope of Watern Tor. An obvious track takes you into the gully of the Wallabrook and up the opposite bank, then on to the summit of the tor, with its distinctive laminated, air-blasted rock stumps.

It is worth pausing on Watern Tor for a well-deserved rest, because here you can shelter from the west wind and gaze down on the extensive plain of the River Teign, its uniformity contrasting with the patchwork of colour on the lowland hills on the eastern horizon. From here you can also look back along the Forest boundary and appreciate how obvious it must have been for the perambulators of 1240 to choose for their boundary line the great backbone of moorland that runs southwards from Cosdon to Hound Tor and on to this unmistakeable landmark.

On leaving Watern Tor, you should continue on a bearing of 129° to Hew Lake Foot, where the little stream of Hew Lake falls into the North Teign. This line takes you across the shoulder of Watern Tor, over the Teignhead Farm enclosure wall and down a steep slope towards the bottom of the river

Watern Tor viewed from the east.

Hew Lake Foot, where Hew Lake (foreground) joins the North Teign.

The Longstone, with Kestor Rock beyond. Note the inscriptions 'GP' (Gidleigh parish) and 'DC' (Duchy of Cornwall).

valley. To the right is a deep combe known as Wood Hole Pit, from where the tiny stream of Hew Lake takes the short journey down the hill and into the North Teign. This confluence was one of the boundary points on the 1240 perambulation and was referred to as Wotesbrokelakesfote, which does not exactly trip off the tongue today, but is a fascinating piece of old language.

At this same point an enclosure boundary crosses the North Teign in the form of three tubular rails spanning between concrete posts and is known naturally enough as 'Rails'. There is also a ford here known as Mangersford by association with Manga Rock, which lies nearby on the hillside on the west side of the river valley. In autumn, at this idyllic and remote place, the colours of the dying grasses, heather, gorse and bracken provide a stunning backdrop to the North Teign as it flows urgently along the valley floor.

Following a bearing of 102° from Hew Lake Foot, you should now cross over the North Teign via the rails (when the river is high) or the boulders on the river bed (when it is low) and climb up the opposite slope of Langridge. To the left of Langridge, a few straggly trees of the Batworthy enclosure can be seen away on the eastern skyline. Behind you is the lozenge shape of Manga Rock on the opposite hill.

From the top of Langridge there is a fine view down into the little valley of the Stonetor Brook. Stone Tor itself, a squat stump of rock, sits on the south side of the valley and is a good example of a decaying tor. A large rockfield lies between it and the brook, as though a giant hand had contemptuously knocked over a large rockpile. In fact, this mass of rocks has found its way down the slope from Stone Tor by the action of rain, frost and gravity over millions of years and it is clear that the tor was once significantly bigger then it is now. Much more recently, some of the rocks around the tor were used to build the Teignhead Farm newtake walls, one of which even incorporates the tor itself into its structure!

Continuing on a bearing of 102°, you approach the next boundary point - The Longstone - over Shovel Down, where there are many intriguing remains of ancient farmsteads, field walls and settlements. On top of the ridge of Shovel Down, Kestor Rock comes into view and a well-worn path is followed down the slope to The Longstone. This is a four-square standing stone inscribed with the letters 'GP' (Gidleigh Parish) on its northern face and 'DC' (Duchy of Cornwall) on its western face. It is believed to be the 'Heigheston' of the 1240 perambulation, although anyone standing next to the stone and looking east could be forgiven for wondering if the perambulators were actually referring to Kestor Rock.

From The Longstone your next destination is the Heath Stone, which lies 1¹/₂ miles away on Chagford Common, next to the Fernworthy Forest access road. Initially, this part of the route involves heading in a straight line from The Longstone to Thornworthy Tor and then walking southwards towards Fernworthy Reservoir until you reach an area of enclosed pastureland. The wall here should then be followed around to the right for a short distance so as to enable you to join the footpath that leads down the side of the valley and skirts the northern shore of the reservoir as far as the dam: at the foot of the dam you will, perhaps, be momentarily transfixed (as I was) by the noise of the overspill and the half-terrifying sensation of standing immediately below a massive body of water. Continuing, the path next leads through narrow gaps between rhododendron bushes, across a footbridge spanning the South Teign and then up the opposite side to the Fernworthy Forest car park, from where a final walk along the metalled public road takes you out of the trees to a rectangular stone set in a low, ruinous boundary wall. Here at last is the Heath Stone.

The Heath Stone is anything but prominent and it is hard to believe that it was significant enough to feature as a boundary point on the 1240 perambulation. In 1970 Sydney Potter, the superintendent of Fernworthy Reservoir, took it upon himself to carve the words 'Jesus said, "I am the way and the life"' on its southern face. When I first visited it I had to walk round it to check for the presence of Sydney Potter's graffiti to confirm that this nondescript, though large, block of stone was indeed the Heath Stone. Although it is not prominent, documentary evidence suggests that the Heath Stone was indeed the 'Langestone' of 1240; more on this in the next chapter.

The Heath Stone, with the road into Fernworthy Forest car park beyond.

2. The Heath Stone to King's Oven – 1.5 miles

Starting point: The car park at Fernworthy Reservoir.
Grid ref: SX 669 839.
Other important information: Clear of all firing ranges.
Total length of walk: Around 3 miles. Best to retrace your steps to return to your car.

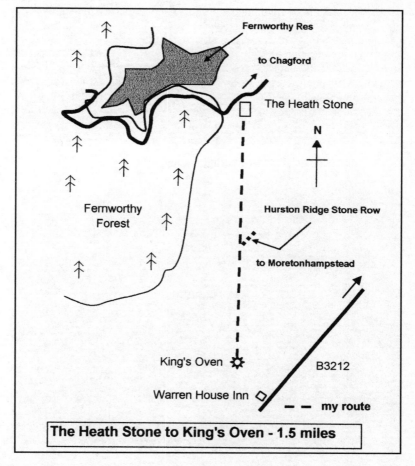

Hurston Ridge stone row.

The King's Oven cairn.

This is a short but significant section of the Forest boundary, lying generally between Fernworthy Forest and The Warren House Inn on the B3212 road. The Heath Stone, as we have seen in the previous chapter, is a rectangular stone adjacent to the road that leads to Fernworthy Reservoir, near the point where the road enters Fernworthy Forest.

You have to head south from the Heath Stone, your route crossing a little ridge, and then over the soft valley floor of the Metheral Brook. Looking west from this valley, Fernworthy Forest caps the high ground of Assycombe Hill, while to the south the tallest stone in the Hurston Ridge Stone Row appears like a lone human figure on the skyline.

This stone row lies immediately to the east of the straight line between the Heath Stone and King's Oven and should be the next destination on this walk, because it is well worth an inspection. It is actually a double stone row over 100 metres in length, with a 'kink' in the last two or three metres at each end. At the southern end, and in the more southerly of the two rows, stands a stone that is head and shoulders above all the others. At the same end a transverse stone seems to have been placed on the ground to define the end of the double row. It is a sobering thought that the passing of the jurors on their mission to define the Forest bounds in 1240 is one of the more recent events witnessed by the Hurston Ridge Stone Row. Perhaps the jurors would have stopped to inspect it, or tethered some of their horses to the single tall stone while pausing from their duties. At any rate they resisted the temptation to use it as a Forest bound, perhaps because it is only prominent from the north: they would no doubt have been aiming to have all the boundary points clearly visible for some distance around, so that no-one could have any excuse for being unaware that their animals had strayed into the Forest.

Short-grazed turf now gives way to the bracken of Hurston Ridge, and from the high point of the ridge can be seen the prominence of Water Hill, on which the summit cairn, King's Oven (known as Furnum Regis in the 1240 record), marks the end of this short stage of the boundary walk. Much stumbling through the heather eventually brings you to this landmark.

As you leave the Heath Stone, the horizons are limited by Hurston Ridge and Fernworthy Forest, and as you travel along this section of the boundary there is the need for constant referral to the map to ensure that you are on course. At no point can you see beyond King's Oven - indeed the place itself is not visible until the last half-mile or so. But what a striking view lies behind, if you turn to look northwards from King's Oven. The span of the whole north-eastern section of the Forest boundary is laid out before you, culminating in Cosdon Hill, 7 miles away, with Kestor Rock intervening prominently. This view provokes much thought; the mind of the traveller journeying clockwise along the boundary is befuddled by speculation about the locations of the old boundary points of Heigheston and Langestone. The prominence of Kestor Rock, as viewed from King's Oven, might suggest that *it* could have been the Heigheston, rather than The Longstone on Shovel Down.

Then there is the credibility of the Heath Stone as the location of 'Langestone' in the record of the 1240 perambulation. It is one of the most insignificant bound marks on the Forest boundary and must either have had some great importance in those days to warrant this special status, or have been the best-placed marker to suit the conclusions of the jurors about the route of the boundary in this area.

Another doubt about the Heath Stone being 'Langestone' centres on the fact that, in the original 1240 list, there are two other boundary points between 'Langestone' and 'Furnum Regis'. These are stated as the 'Turbariam [Turbary] of Alberysheved' and 'Wallebroke'. It seems implausible that, with generally such long distances between most boundary points, there should be a need for two intermediate points over the short distance of around $1^1/2$ miles between the Heath Stone and King's Oven. Moreover, the names do not appear to relate to any features on the ground over this section of the boundary; it has, in fact, been suggested that the mention of Wallebroke was an inadvertent repetition of a name mentioned later in the translated description of the boundary.

In volume 2 of *Dartmoor Atlas of Antiquities* Dr Jeremy Butler speculates that the single prominent stone of the Hurston Ridge Stone Row (see above) is a strong candidate for the 'Langestone' of 1240. This is feasible, although it would seem odd to have this bound point so close (just over half a mile) to the next one at King's Oven.

The 1608 perambulation record contains a reference to 'Yessestone' and William Crossing, in *Echoes of an Ancient Forest*, states that this was an alternative reading of 'Langestone', although he does not state the source of his information. So it is quite conceivable that the 1240 boundary passed through, or close to, a stone whose name could easily have been corrupted to Heath Stone over the intervening centuries.

Moreover, in challenging these widely accepted identities, it has to be conceded that the 1608 boundary was generally a refinement rather than a radical re-routing of the 1240 boundary. This was probably because the identity of the 1240 bound points had been widely disseminated over the centuries by word of mouth throughout the local Dartmoor communities - after all, the position of the Forest boundary was a significant influence in the daily lives of graziers and farmers who farmed the border commons of Dartmoor. Indeed, the 1608 jurors confirmed at the Survey Court that they had defined the Forest bounds partly from copies of ancient records, partly upon the evidence of other persons and partly upon their own knowledge, but especially as the bounds 'have been and are used and are accustomed to be these...'.

If the identity of the Heath Stone as Langestone is controversial, then the location of King's Oven at the southern end of the walk has also been the subject of debate. It is nowadays accepted that King's Oven is the cairn on the top of Water Hill, behind the Warren House Inn. However, the 2002 Ordnance Survey (OS) Explorer map No. OL28 shows King's Oven as an enclosed area 400 or so metres east of the Water Hill cairn, perpetuating a view held by eminent Dartmoor experts such as Robert Burnard, Richard Hansford Worth and William Crossing. Yet the first edition (1809) of the OS 1 inch to 1 mile map shows King's Oven as being the cairn on Water Hill. Samuel Rowe, in *A Perambulation of the Antient and Royal Forest of Dartmoor and the Venville Precincts* (first published in 1848), accepts the Water Hill location for King's Oven, as do the Rev. E. A. Bray (1831) and John Lloyd Warden Page (1889). It is ironic that the latter two authors propounded the correct location given the mockery directed at some of their ideas by William Crossing, the paragon of Dartmoor writers.

The enclosure wrongly named King's Oven appears to be the remains of a prehistoric enclosure, containing traces of prehistoric structures, tinners' pits and other more minor features. It is clearly of interest, but is not a Forest boundary marker.[1]

Whatever the truth, it is fascinating to try to put yourself in the position of the twelve jurors and follow their thought processes as they deliberated over the landscape. Whatever the exact detail of the route may have been, there is no doubt that inside the line lies the high moor, while on the other side the land falls away to the Dartmoor lowlands. Was there some kind of benevolence guiding their ministrations as they bestowed upon the common man as much of the good, less exposed grazing land as they could? Or was it simply that the hunting was better on the high moor?

In the next stage, southwards from King's Oven, the boundary follows a route over which no arguments or theories are necessary. From here the twelve jurors, perhaps tiring for a while of defining straight lines between points on the moor which were not always visible one to the other, opted to follow watercourses - real, not imaginary, lines on the ground - for the next 8 miles.

Continuing in their footsteps, the walker can see how the descent from King's Oven marks a very significant change in the landscape of the Forest boundary. For next there comes a departure from the exposed high moor into the more sheltered central basin of Dartmoor, where we will make our way on another day.

[1] I have referred in these paragraphs to Dr Tom Greeves' article 'King Arthur's Oven - Dartmoor's First Tourist Attraction?', published in *Dartmoor Magazine*, issue no.39, summer 1995.

3. King's Oven to Pizwell – 1.9 miles

Starting point: The car park just east of the Warren House Inn, on the south side of the B3212 (but not outside or near the pub itself - leave that area for the pub's customers).
Grid ref: SX 676 811.
Other important information: Clear of all firing ranges.
Total length of walk: Around 4 miles. Best to retrace your steps to return to your car.

The 1240 Forest boundary leaves King's Oven and descends Water Hill, crossing what is now the B3212 road about 200 metres east of The Warren House Inn, to reach the head of the Wallabrook. The boundary now follows this stream from its head over its whole length of 4¾ miles to its confluence with the East Dart.

A convenient point from which to begin the walk along this section of the boundary is the car park east of The Warren House Inn, from where you can climb up to King's Oven and then descend to Wallabrook Head, to the south of the road. It is always fascinating to see the tiny trickle that gives birth to a Dartmoor stream. In most cases the stream and its valley both grow in size as

The view down the Wallabrook valley from near The Warren House Inn.

the water descends its course. Oddly though, in the case of the Wallabrook, whilst the valley becomes much deeper, the stream itself does not increase markedly in width over its entire course.

Follow the Wallabrook downstream along its right bank. You will find yourself dropping rapidly as the ground falls away from the road. Soon the route goes along the top of a steep bank above a deep channel that appears to be partly natural from water action and partly artificial from the efforts of the tinners. Everywhere in this little valley are the remains of tin workings, in the form of streamings, or piles of small rocks discarded after the tin ore had been separated from them by the action of water. In many places these streamings are now grassed over, and in the channel itself a number of trees have established themselves. High on the hill above you to the right is The Warren

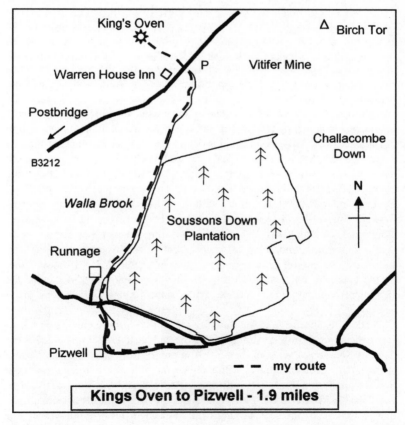

Kings Oven to Pizwell - 1.9 miles

House Inn, a very different view to that which the driver on the B3212 is accustomed to seeing.

Soon you reach the dark and gloomy conifer trees of Soussons Plantation on the left bank of the stream, and it is noticeable how the initially rapid fall of the Wallabrook becomes more placid as the gradient levels out. The atmosphere here is almost claustrophobic, often with dampness in the air, with all those coniferous clones bearing down on you. This is a very different sensation from what you experience while walking the Forest boundary over the high moor.

Continue to follow the Wallabrook downstream on its right bank, crossing the remains of an old enclosure wall before floundering, perhaps, through what can be very wet ground. Then pick your way through an increasing number of gorse bushes until you reach the walled, wire-topped enclosure of Runnage Farm. At this point it is easier to cross to the left bank of the Wallabrook and follow the narrow strip of bank between the stream and the wall of Soussons Plantation. It is barely possible to get through this section of the walk, especially when the ground is wet, but the journey becomes easier again when a small clapper bridge over the Wallabrook is reached, opposite Runnage Farm.

Runnage is the one of the ancient tenements that lie near the Forest boundary. Occupied by the Coaker family since 1843, it is first mentioned in documents from 1304/05 and its history is not without incident; in the late 1700s one John Stock was murdered there and, in 1868 or thereabouts, the old tenement was destroyed by fire. It is possible that Runnage existed at the time of the 1240 perambulation; if so, it would have been part of the parish of Lydford and its inhabitants, along with those from other tenements, such as Pizwell, Sherwell and Babeny, would have had to make the long journey along the Lich Path across the moor to Lydford whenever they had to bury a dead relative or friend. This arduous obligation finally terminated in 1260 following a successful petition of the Bishop of Exeter, Walter Bronescombe, by the tenement holders. From then on they were permitted to receive the sacrament and bury their dead at Widecombe Church, which was much nearer.

A short distance beyond the Runnage clapper bridge you emerge into open space by the road from Postbridge to Cator. And what a relief it is to leave the trees of Soussons Plantation behind! It is one of only two (the other being Fernworthy) close encounters with conifers on the entire journey around the Forest boundary. I find the Fernworthy, Bellever and Soussons plantations wholly out of place in the Dartmoor landscape. Yet it must be remembered that commercial forestry provides much-needed local employment for Dartmoor people; moreover, the conifer plantations have become established habitats for an abundance of wildlife.

28

Runnage Bridge, looking north, with Runnage Farm to the left and Soussons Plantation to the right.

Pizwell Farm, with the Wallabrook and stepping stones.

After walking across the nearby Runnage Bridge turn left almost immediately and proceed for a quarter of a mile along a metalled track to another ancient tenement, Pizwell. A pleasant, narrow swathe of ground lies between the track and the Wallabrook and, if you are a purist boundary walker, you can leave the track and follow the brook along its right bank. At Pizwell the public right of way meets the Church Way, which runs from east to west and crosses the Wallabrook at a ford. Across this ford is a set of stepping-stones which, with their backcloth of the old farm buildings of Pizwell, make a much-photographed, idyllic Dartmoor farm scene.

Pizwell, as already stated, is another of the ancient tenements of Dartmoor and the earliest known documentary reference to it is in a 1260 register of Walter Bronescombe, Bishop of Exeter. As with Runnage, it almost certainly existed at the time of the 1240 perambulation, so one can speculate about the reaction of the occupants of these two farms as the twelve knights and their entourage rode up on their historic task. Would they have been so bold as to attempt to influence the decisions of the knights? In all likelihood, they did not - recent memory of draconian Forest laws and the fact that those knights were many social strata above the tenement holders probably deterred them from approaching the party voluntarily. However, as local farmers, they might well have been questioned by the knights about their use of the land and the duration of their occupation of the tenements, as part of the fact-finding required to fix the boundary in this area.

It would have been as clear to the 1240 jurors as it is to us today that this part of Dartmoor is lower in altitude, less exposed to the elements and more conducive to farming than many other parts of the Forest. What we do not know about, of course, is their attitude to the needs of land users other than the king, or the instructions that were given to them by the Sheriff of Devon as to the principles that should guide them in the task of fixing the Forest boundary. It is interesting to look at the map and note that, had the aim simply been to place as much as possible of the higher parts of the moor in the Forest, then the boundary would have followed first the lower ground east of Shapley Down and then the East Webburn, some 3 miles to the east. However, the intervening ground contains not only higher moorland, such as Hameldon, but also a significant amount of lower, sheltered ground that lends itself to agriculture. It is a comforting thought that the knights may have been guided by the high principle of fairness to other land users when they fixed the Forest boundary, both here at the Wallabrook and elsewhere on the moor.

4. Pizwell to Dartmeet – 3.9 miles

Starting point: Park off the road at Runnage Bridge.
Grid ref: SX 668 789.
Other important information: The actual 1240 boundary (the Wallabrook) is partly within private land, so cannot be accessed in some parts.
Total length of walk: Around 8 miles. Best to retrace your steps to return to your car.

Southwards from Pizwell the Forest boundary, still coincident with the Wallabrook, passes across enclosed land forming part of Cator Common. You therefore have to seek the nearest public right of way and this is found by following the Church Way eastwards from the ford across the Wallabrook at Pizwell for about 500 metres. Then you take a track that heads southwards and after a mile or so the road from Bellever to Cator is reached.

It has to be said that the Forest boundary immediately south of Pizwell is perhaps the least scenic of any part on the circumference. It comprises enclosed agricultural land and it is not permissible to walk along the banks of the Wallabrook. We should not complain too much about this but instead should remember that this is part of the central, lower lying basin of Dartmoor where farming has established a rightful foothold. Indeed, agricultural operations based at Pizwell and Runnage have been practised here for very many centuries, as attested to by the multitude of small walled fields that stretch from Pizwell right across to Postbridge.

To the south of the Bellever to Cator road, the Wallabrook skirts accessible land for about half a mile before entering enclosed land once more. Consequently, it is now necessary to deviate from the Forest boundary somewhat, and a suggested route is as follows:-

Leave the Bellever to Cator Road by Riddon Brake and walk southwards, parallel with the Wallabrook, but about 250 metres up the slope to the west of the stream. There is every good reason for this, because the ground on the floor of this part of the Wallabrook valley is very soft and boggy. Even then you may still encounter soft ground some way up the slope, and I can say with certainty that it is best to get as far up Riddon Ridge as possible in order to make any reasonable headway.

The view from near the top of the ridge is quite interesting in its contrasts; on the east bank of the Wallabrook the landscape is one of enclosed agricultural land, with the long straight belts of trees known as Grendon Strips being the most prominent features. These were planted in the 1860s to provide shelter from the westerly wind for the higher ground between the

The bridge over the Wallabrook at Riddon Brake, with Soussons Plantation beyond.

Wallabrook and the West Webburn. To the south-west, Laughter Tor crowns the hilltop above the Bellever Plantation. Riddon Ridge itself is something of an intrusion of high, open moorland among surroundings of enclosed walled fields.

Now make for the southernmost corner of the open land of Riddon Ridge. According to Eric Hemery in *High Dartmoor*, Riddon is a shortening of 'Red Down', a name having its origins in the colour of the late summer heather that then thrived here. Passing a low wall, you join a branch of the ancient Lich Path, along which, prior to 1260, the inhabitants of Sherwell and Babeny carried their dead to Lydford for burial. A short walk of a few hundred metres then leads you into the farmyard of Babeny, another ancient tenement. In the distance looms the massive profile of Yar Tor, filling the view to the south. In the farmyard itself, a miscellany of geese, peacocks and hens pecks and picks over the hard stony ground.

Continue downhill along the Lich Path, which has by now become a metalled road, and descend from the farmyard to Babeny Bridge.

An alternative route from Riddon Brake to Babeny Bridge initially entails a brisk climb eastwards up the metalled road from the nearby cattle grid, which takes you over the high point of Cator Common, through one of the Grendon Strips and on past walled fields to a T-junction. At this point the road

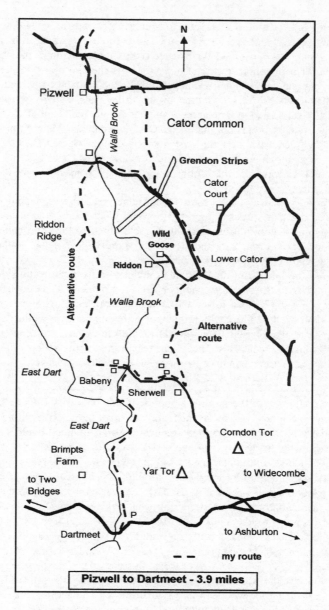

Reproduced by permission of Ordnance Survey on behalf of The Controller of Her Majesty's Stationery Office, © Crown Copyright 100042123.

branching off to the north-east leads to Middle Cator (formerly the domain of the late Lady Sylvia Sayer) and Great Cator before meandering into and out of the West Webburn valley. However, you should continue past this T-junction for about another quarter of a mile with the aim of staying close to the Forest boundary, still defined hereabouts by the Wallabrook, which lies in the valley to your right. Down there on the valley floor are two farms called Wild Goose and Riddon. The latter is another ancient tenement of the Forest, although Hemery points out that the earliest documentary mention of it is in 1488 - two centuries after the first mention of Pizwell and Babeny. Wild Goose, located on the site of a previous farm known as Cator Cot, lies in the parish of Widecombe-in-the-Moor, on the opposite bank of the Wallabrook from Riddon.

To make your way back towards the Wallabrook leave the metalled road by going down the track signposted to Wild Goose and Riddon and then turning immediately left along another track which follows the contour of Corndon Down. From here the steepness of the valley of the Wallabrook between Riddon and Babeny is striking.

Cross the heath and then scramble down a stony path leading through gorse bushes to Sherwell, yet another ancient tenement. The silhouettes of Corndon Tor and Yar Tor tower above this old settlement, with the metalled access road winding like a white ribbon over the saddle between the two high points. At Sherwell itself is an ancient-looking farmyard - a scene that has barely changed in centuries. Then a chattering stream, the waters of the Shir Well that gave the settlement its name, accompanies you as you continue down the road to Babeny Bridge.

The final stage of the journey along the Forest boundary from Pizwell to Dartmeet is characterised by an enchanting blend of trees and tumbling water. After the Wallabrook has swirled amongst the well-rounded boulders on its bed at Babeny Bridge, it continues southwards over a tract of flat, open ground studded with gorse and blackthorn bushes. The stream itself is bounded on both sides by small trees, through which a path can be followed along either bank. If you stay on the east side you soon reach a little clapper bridge, a superlative artefact straddling what remains a narrow stream, even this far below its head.

A short distance below the clapper bridge, the Wallabrook finally yields its independence and flows into the East Dart. The boundary of the Forest does likewise. Across the river a row of stepping stones serves, except in times of spate, to carry the walker high and dry to the opposite bank, from where a footpath leads up the wooded hillside to Brimpts Farm and beyond. Stay on the left bank of the East Dart and follow it through the valley floor landscape. First you come to a small cluster of trees that give shade to a collection of moss-encrusted boulders, reminiscent of the interior of Black-a-Tor Copse on

The clapper bridge over the Wallabrook south of Babeny.

Stepping stones over the East Dart for the path up to Brimpts Farm.

the northern moor. Next, by contrast, comes a very pleasant open area of green, level turf, which, with little sandy beaches at the river's edge, forms a natural picnic site for those who walk upstream from Dartmeet in summer. All the while, to your left, the slopes of Yar Tor sweep upwards and away to another world on the hilltop far above.

All too soon you will be approaching Badger's Holt and walking down the footpath into Dartmeet car park. To complete the walk the purist should cross the road and walk the few metres to the point where the West Dart and East Dart unite.

The 6 miles of the Forest boundary from King's Oven to Dartmeet are an unusual Dartmoor experience. The land here is cultivated and inhabited, but as much a part of Dartmoor's history as the open uplands. In the next chapter you will discover that, 2 miles further on beyond Dartmeet, you reach the exposed hills again as you continue to follow the course charted by the Henry III's jurors more than 760 years ago.

Dartmeet, with the East Dart in the right foreground.

———— 5. Dartmeet to Ryder's Hill – 3.1 miles ————

Starting point: The car park at Dartmeet.
Grid ref: SX 672 733.
Other important information: Here, part of the 1240 Forest boundary (the banks of the West Dart and the lower reaches of the O Brook) lies within enclosed land and cannot be accessed. In addition, if the stepping stones at Dartmeet are submerged, it is a good indicator that those at Week Ford are also under water and are therefore unsafe to cross. In such circumstances proceed instead as far as Huccaby Farm (as described below), then follow the road through Hexworthy to rejoin the Forest boundary at Saddle Bridge.
Total length of walk: Around 6 miles, depending on your choice of return route.

From the car park at Dartmeet walk across the bridge and down beside the houses on the south side of the road into a field beside the West Dart River. The first leg of the Forest boundary from Dartmeet follows the West Dart upstream to the confluence of the O Brook by Week Ford. However, as this part of the river runs through enclosed land, you will have to walk along the public footpath that goes uphill from Dartmeet in a north-westerly direction.

At the top of the field, the path takes you between moss-encrusted stone walls and out on to the level ground of the hilltop. It then makes a right-angled turn to the left, or south-west, passes between short timber posts painted yellow and continues for about a quarter of a mile on a route that converges on the road to Hexworthy. Along the way, from this quite elevated position, you have a good view southwards towards your destination - the high ground of the southern moor and Ryder's Hill itself. Before long, though, you will have almost reached the road to Hexworthy and be entering Huccaby farmyard, where a track to the left, which you should now join, leads off towards Week Ford. Below this track, to the right, is St Raphael's Church and soon there is a fine view of Hexworthy, with Down Ridge beyond it.

Continue to follow the track as it curves to the left and downhill towards the West Dart. Soon you will reach Week Ford, where a series of substantial stepping stones will take you across to the other side of the river - provided that it is not in spate! After heavy rain the West Dart will be brown in colour with standing waves generated by the high flow: the stepping stones will be submerged and any attempt to cross them would be suicidal, because anyone falling into the river in such conditions is more than likely to drown. If you are in doubt about attempting to cross the river, and certainly if the stepping stones are under water, you should retrace your steps to Huccaby farmyard

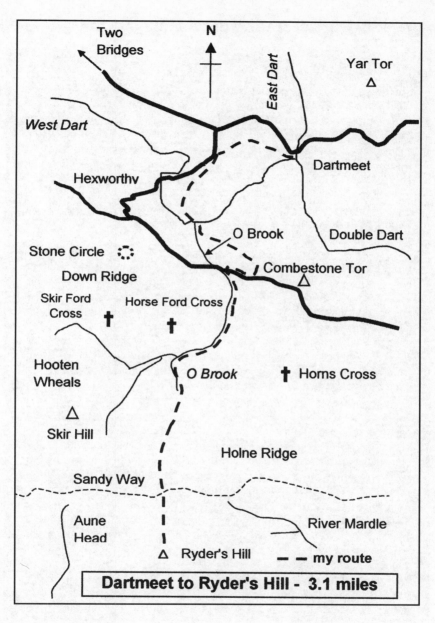

Reproduced by permission of Ordnance Survey on behalf of The Controller of Her Majesty's Stationery Office, © Crown Copyright 100042123.

Stepping stones over the O Brook near Week Ford.

and then walk along the road from Huccaby Farm through Hexworthy to Saddle Bridge on the O Brook.

However, if the Week Ford stepping stones are not submerged, and you are confident enough to do so, cross carefully and continue along the right bank of the river until you meet the O Brook coming down through the trees from the right. Here there are more stepping stones, but the crossing is much less hazardous as the O Brook is only a few metres wide at this spot. Then follow the worn track up the hill to the east until you meet the metalled track to Combestone Farm. Turn right and in a short distance you will come to the road from Hexworthy to Holne. At this point, turn right again towards Hexworthy and, at the bottom of the hill, you will come to Saddle Bridge over the O Brook. At the bridge, you must turn south-eastwards off the road to follow the Forest boundary once more, alongside the O Brook.

Although the O Brook is much smaller than the West Dart and plainly carries less water, it often seems to be in a much angrier mood. After heavy rain it captures a lot of water from Down Ridge, Skir Hill and Holne Ridge, and bubbles, tumbles and roars its way down the hill. Moreover, the ground next to the O Brook can be quite soft, resulting in a rather tiring uphill slog, but the antics of the running water make the journey more tolerable.

The rough and tumble of the O Brook above Saddle Bridge.

Eventually you come to the site of Horse Ford, where you must cross the Wheal Emma Leat. This leat once conveyed water along an ingeniously-routed course of gradual descent around the contours from the River Swincombe at Fox Tor Mire for 8 miles to the Mardle valley. Here it supplemented the waters of the River Mardle in driving the waterwheels used in the tin workings by the river.

Some four hundred metres further upstream you will reach Dry Lake Foot, the confluence of the tiny stream called Dry Lake with the O Brook. At this point one is struck by the contrast between the great straight-line sweeps of the Forest boundary across other parts of the moor with the fastidiously detailed choice of route here, following streams uphill as far as possible towards top of Ryder's Hill. Nevertheless, there was much logic in the route chosen by the knights of 1240. Ryder's Hill has a huge, gradually rounded profile and it is easy to miss the summit even in clear weather unless a compass and map are used. Probably there was never any doubt that a place as prominent as Ryder's Hill would be on the boundary, but, facing similar problems to walkers today, those twelve knights must surely have wanted to ensure that the route of the Forest boundary was unambiguous as far as possible towards the summit, which cannot actually be seen until one is 200 metres or so away from it. The simplest way to achieve the desired clarity of position was to make use of rivers and streams as much as possible.

Carry on up the broad shallow gully through the centre of which flows Dry Lake. There are many tin-streaming heaps on the gully floor and some of them must be extremely old, for this area was known as Dryework - literally 'the workings of Dry Lake' - in 1240, when the Forest boundary was first perambulated. At the top of the gully is a solitary tree containing the abandoned nest of a crow or raven, almost the last clear landmark before the summit of Ryder's Hill and a good place to pause for lunch or a drink. From here you will have a fine view to the hills of northern Dartmoor and of Fernworthy Forest wrapping itself over White Ridge and Assycombe Hill just to the east of Sittaford Tor.

On picking your way out of the gully of Dry Lake, you will find that you are now on more featureless terrain, where the only detail seems to be endless swathes of long grass. You can now either guess the direction to follow or, preferably, use your compass to send you on a bearing of 187° for a point known in 1240 as Dryfeldford - nowadays taken to be the point where the boundary crosses the Sandy Way (a track that leads from Michelcombe up on to the high moor, terminating at the site of the old turf ties around Swincombe Head). A faint footpath can sometimes be discerned across what is often bleak, windswept grassland and soon you are crossing the Sandy Way, from where you need to walk on a revised bearing of 180°.

Next, unless it is foggy, you will see a line of stones that mark the boundary between Holne parish and the Forest. Follow this and then, after making your way up over a sharper rise, you should finally be able to see and reach the stones on the summit of Ryder's Hill. Of these, the largest is a typical Ordnance Survey triangulation stone, with the usual brass mounting

Summit stones on Ryder's Hill.

for a theodolite cast into its flat top. The next largest is a slightly leaning, rough-cut stone, rectangular in cross-section and with the letter 'B' carved on its eastern face. It is known as Petre's Boundstone and the inscription denotes the parish of Buckfastleigh. The smallest stone, a replica of the original and inscribed 'H' to denote the boundary between the parish of Holne and the Forest, is known as Petre-on-the-Mount.

Ryder's Hill is one of the most prominent points on the Forest boundary yet, at 515 metres above sea level, it is of lower elevation than a number of the boundary points on the northern moor. For instance, Rattlebrook Head and Cosdon Hill are both at 550 metres and Watern Tor is at 526 metres. There is nonetheless a stunning view from Ryder's Hill and it is said that, on a clear day, you can see beyond Teignmouth as far east as Portland Bill.

I well remember walking this section of the boundary with my wife in April 2000 because, once we had reached Ryder's Hill, the heavens opened and we endured continuous pouring rain all the way back via Hensroost Mine through Hexworthy to Dartmeet. We in fact reached the point where our clothes could not get any wetter and arrived back at the Dartmeet car park well and truly drenched, having to tip a large amount of water from our boots. But every uncomfortable Dartmoor walk has its compensations. First came the pleasure of changing into dry clothes, then a pot of tea in front of the fire at The Plume of Feathers in Princetown. Finally, we headed for our overnight destination at the Cherrybrook Hotel for a shower, more hot tea, a fine meal and a sound sleep. This was not exactly reliving the conditions experienced by the 1240 perambulators - but then, authenticity can only be carried so far!

——6. Ryder's Hill to Erme Head – 5.8 miles——

Starting point: Park at the side of the road leading to Lud Gate, without obstructing it.
Grid ref: SX 693 672.
Total length of walk: Around 12 miles. From Erme Head the shortest way back to Lud Gate is to retrace your steps to Red Lake Foot, then head up Red Lake to Crossways, down to Huntingdon Cross and upstream alongside the Western Wellabrook. On reaching the track from Lud Gate, follow this back to your car.

Having parked at the side of the road leading to Lud Gate, continue to the gate itself and out on to the open moor. Ryder's Hill can then be reached by walking along the ridge via Pupers Hill and Snowdon.

From the summit of Ryder's Hill the broad, well-worn path back to Snowdon is prominent, but your route lies to the right of this track and you should set off on a bearing of 138° so as to meet the gully at the head of Western Wellabrook. The ground is usually wet here and you may well find yourself having to flounder along, trying to avoid the more obvious soft spots. At the entrance to the gully is a standing stone, inscribed with the letter 'B' to

The boundstone at the head of Wellabrook Gert, with Eastern Whitebarrow to the right on the skyline.

44

denote the meeting of the boundary of Buckfastleigh parish with the Forest boundary. From being perched high on the open, exposed shoulder of Ryder's Hill, you now descend into the enclosed shelter of Wellabrook Gert. All the way down this gully are piles of streamings left by the tinners of bygone years. After picking your way around the side slopes - to avoid wet ground in the bottom of the gert - the view ahead opens up to reveal, in the distance, the site of Huntingdon Warren House, marked by a lone sycamore tree. Above it towers Eastern Whitebarrow, looking much higher than it does from the top

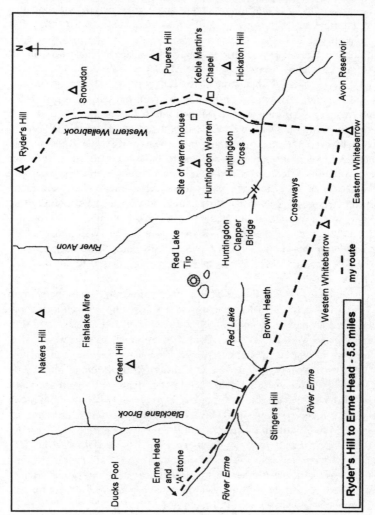

of Ryder's Hill. It is a reminder of the hard work that will come later!

When you leave Wellabrook Gert, the valley opens out and, as you approach the enclosures of Huntingdon Warren, which were restored and topped with wire in 1996, you cross the track that comes over Pupers Hill from Lud Gate. At the southern end of the warren enclosures the gradient of the Western Wellabrook becomes steeper as it starts its final descent to the Avon. By now, Eastern Whitebarrow fills the southern sky and there could not have been much doubt in the minds of the twelve jurors that their line would soon have to leave the streams and rivers that had marked the route for most of the previous 11 miles from Wallabrook Head and make for the lofty summit far above.

Huntingdon Warren House has an interesting history. The warren itself dates from 1808, being established by the Michelmore family, and includes some 700 acres of land. Numerous artificial burrows, shown as 'pillow mounds' on the OS map, were constructed to house the rabbits. Some years later the two-storey house was built on the eastern side of the hill, sheltered from the prevailing (and wet) westerly winds. However, Huntingdon Warren never established the brisk trading of Trowlesworthy, Ditsworthy and Headland Warrens and, moreover, appears to have been raided illicitly for rabbit meat by the various moorland workers who found themselves nearby - the peat cutters of Red Lake and, much later, the workers at the Red Lake China Clay Works. Indeed, when the china clay working began in 1913 at Red Lake, the warrener, John (Jan) Waye, took a regular job there to supplement his meagre income from the warren. The warren ceased to operate just after World War 1 and the Waye family, after John had worked at a number of jobs and his wife had taken in paying guests, finally left the house in the early 1940s.

In 1942 a recluse called Frederick William Symes moved into the warren house. He was the son of a Methodist minister and a former schoolteacher and was aged around 70 when he took up his hermit-like existence at this remote spot. He would live there during the summer and in lodgings at Buckfastleigh in winter. In summer he spent much of his time roaming the moor, and twice weekly would walk a 12-mile return shopping journey to Buckfastleigh. He renamed the house 'The Lone Stead', and by all accounts hygiene and cleanliness did not feature high on his list of household priorities! He received a twice-weekly postal visit, apparently resorting to writing letters to himself to make sure that the service continued!

In thick fog on the afternoon of Saturday, 13th October 1945 an American Dakota aircraft crashed near the northern boundary of Huntingdon Warren, killing all seven American crew on board and scattering wreckage. Symes later retrieved one or two items, including a propeller, to decorate the otherwise much-neglected interior of the house.

Symes endured this existence until 1956 when, at the age of 84, he left the house for the last time and moved first to Buckfastleigh and then to Kingsteignton, where he died in 1961. Just after Symes' departure from it, the house was accidentally gutted by a fire that went out of control in an upstairs room during occupancy by a group of naval cadets. The Duchy of Cornwall demolished the remaining ruins in 1961.[1]

Continuing down the Western Wellabrook on its left bank, you reach the remains of the rough stone 'chapel' constructed by the Reverend Keble Martin, his brother Arthur and some of their friends when they camped nearby in 1909. The structure was never roofed and comprises a small hollow lined with stones to form crude walls, and a cross, inscribed by Arthur Martin, on a stone at the northern end. Keble Martin later found fame as the author of *Concise British Flora in Colour*. Around the 'chapel' are the remains of the New Huntingdon Tin Mine, including a fairly intact building which once housed a waterwheel that pumped water from the workings.

Beyond the mine building the Western Wellabrook descends around the flank of Huntingdon Hill and, as you continue to walk downstream, a cave-like formation of large boulders will be seen high up on the hillside. A natural feature, this is a place where one or two sheep like to shelter in very bad, or very hot, weather. Below you, meanwhile, the valley of the Wellabrook now starts to open out into that of the Avon and before long you will find yourself at Wellabrook Foot - just south of Huntingdon Cross, and the point at which the waters of the Wellabrook and Avon unite. The cross, incidentally, was not erected until some 300 years after the perambulation of 1240 and marks the boundary of lands held by Buckfast Abbey prior to the Dissolution of the Monasteries.

When you reach this spot the immediate problem is how to cross to the other side of the Avon, as the river is sufficiently wide to make the task difficult. The easier, but longer, option is to walk upstream to the Huntingdon clapper bridge. However, as it did in my case, sheer laziness may prompt you to attempt to cross the river by stepping precariously across the tops of some conveniently placed, albeit rather slippery, rocks!

Now comes the moment for an all-out assault on the slope of Eastern Whitebarrow. In fact, the climb proves to be easier than it looks, particularly if you take a very slow pace up the steepest parts. The gradient starts off steep, then eases for a while before becoming steeper again on the final approach to the summit. On arrival, you will be confronted by the strange spectacle of the barrow itself, which was measured by William Crossing as 36 feet high and 270 feet in circumference. Stop here for a well-earned rest and absorb a panoramic view of your surroundings.

Taking a first scan of the view from Eastern Whitebarrow is like climbing a stepladder to look out over the roof of a house. It is situated on the edge of

Eastern Whitebarrow.

the high moor; to the south, the ground falls away rapidly to the Avon valley, Brent Moor and down to the lowlands beyond South Brent. But to the north there is an exceptional view into the very heart of the southern moor - Great Mis Tor, North Hessary Tor and Red Lake spoil tip are prominent, while Aune Head can be seen through the gap between the hills on either side of the Avon. To the south-west is Knattabarrow, with Three Barrows beyond. In the east, on the slopes of Dean Moor, are a number of prominent settlement enclosures and, nearer to hand, you can see the line of a former leat on the western slope of Huntingdon Hill. This leat took its water from the Avon above Broad Falls and then went round the side of the hill to supply Huntingdon Warren House.

Eastern Whitebarrow as a Forest boundary point has two curious aspects. First, although it is the southernmost point on the boundary, it is some 5 miles from the southern edge of the open moor at Bittaford whereas other boundary points are - with only a few exceptions - closer to the edge of the commons. Consequently, this again begs the question as to what principles guided the decisions of the twelve jurors; they could quite easily have taken in additional land by taking the boundary further south along the Avon and then by following a course to Eylesbarrow via Three Barrows, Stalldon and Langcombe Hill. As I have previously speculated, one possible reason is that the jurors felt that they should in some way take into account the grazing needs of local farmers; another more pragmatic reason might be that they were trying to exclude the deep, steep-sided Erme valley from the Forest on the grounds that it presented a rather formidable barrier to horsemen in pursuit of deer.

The second curious aspect of Eastern Whitebarrow as a boundary point is that the boundary seems to have been purposely extended to include it. A smoother line could have been achieved by taking it from Wellabrook Foot, up over Western Whitebarrow and directly to the head of Red Lake. It would, though, be wholly understandable that the jurors might have wanted to include this very high, prominent landmark to mark the boundary to any grazier putting his animals out on to the southernmost commons. Interestingly, Western Whitebarrow was not specifically named as a Forest boundary point until 1608, although there has always been a local school of thought that Western, not Eastern, Whitebarrow was the intended bound. This seems rather hard to justify - 'Ester Whyteburghe' (the name in the copy of the 1240 text describing the bounds) seems fairly unambiguous.

After your exertions in getting up to the top of the ridge you can now enjoy a pleasant level walk of around a mile to Western Whitebarrow. This barrow had once contained an erect stone cross, but it was desecrated in about 1847 by peat cutters working nearby on the peat-ties that supplied a naphtha works at Shipley Bridge, on the Avon. The stone cross, believed to have been erected on the barrow in 1557, had its arms amputated and was embedded next to a crude hut fashioned by the peat cutters within the stones forming the barrow.

The view from Western Whitebarrow is similar to that from its companion, with the notable exception that, from this point near the southernmost part of the boundary, you can, on a clear day, see Cosdon Hill, the northernmost part, which lies 16 miles away.

In the 1240 perambulation the next boundary point was the confluence of the stream known as Red Lake with the River Erme. To reach it from Western Whitebarrow (situated very close to the notional straight line from Eastern Whitebarrow to that confluence) you should now set off on a bearing of 290° and proceed across the trackbed of the former Zeal Tor Tramway, which had been built in 1847 to convey peat dug out from the area now occupied by the remains of Red Lake China Clay Works down to the naphtha works at Shipley Bridge. (After these operations ceased in 1850, the tramway was re-opened in the late 1870s to transport materials to the short-lived china clay works at Petre's Pit.) From the trackbed continue past the remains of two sand traps that were built to remove sand from the china clay slurry extracted from Red Lake Works. On your route now - and just down the slope from the sand traps - are the extensive remains of the so-called Greenhill Micas; these formed a system of settling tanks that removed mica from the china clay slurry, which then flowed by gravity down twin clayware pipes to drying sheds at Cantrell, near Bittaford.

In this immediate area, as well as the remnants of the china clay and peat industries, the map shows the so-called Abbots' Way[2], a path reputedly (but probably mostly in the imaginations of some early Dartmoor writers!) used by monks to journey from Buckfast Abbey to Buckland or Tavistock abbeys. The point where the Zeal Tor Tramway meets this path is known as Crossways, which I have found to be one of the best places for photographing the Red Lake spoil tip. Although the tip is really just a pile of surplus material from the deep, now water-filled china clay excavations (which should really have been put back in them when the works closed in 1932), it is a weird, almost mystical landmark on the southern moor. Back in 1996, while taking photographs for my book *Escape to Dartmoor!*, I came out to this spot with a tripod and camera. I set everything up and aimed at the Red Lake spoil tip with a modest amount of 'zoom'. More by luck than anything else I ended up with a picture, reproduced on page 36 of *Escape to Dartmoor!*, that sums up the visual impact of the tip - a stark and bleak intrusion on an otherwise anonymous sweep of open plateau.

From the Greenhill Micas you need to continue following the same bearing of 290° and proceed across the nearby trackbed of another former tramway, this one having been designed by Richard Hansford Worth and built in 1912 to convey men and materials between Cantrell and the Red Lake China Clay Works. Thereafter, as you begin to descend the slope of Brown Heath, the ground becomes appreciably rougher and you will find yourself walking through thick grass and occasionally stumbling over large tussocks. This, in turn, may make navigation difficult, but you should now be aiming almost directly towards a single boulder situated to the right of the scarred and eroded area on the slope of Stingers Hill, on the opposite side of the valley.

As you drop down towards the valley floor of the River Erme, the route takes you over the line of the Erme Stone Row, a 1¼-mile line of small stones which project from the ground like ancient teeth as they trace a route from Green Hill on the north side of the Erme valley to The Dancers stone circle away to the south. Shortly afterwards you finally reach an area of short, dark spiky grass where Red Lake flows down from the east into the Erme.

To continue along the boundary of the Forest, you now need to cross Red Lake just above the marshy area at its confluence with the Erme and then turn westwards to follow the river upstream. Take the path that can be clearly seen on the short, well-grazed turf above the north bank of the river. The adjacent slopes of Green Hill provide some of the best grazing on the entire moor as will, no doubt, be exemplified by the presence of many sheep and cattle nearby. Meanwhile, as you continue upstream, the path leads you past the entrances to the valleys of Dry Lake and the Blacklane Brook and on towards the prominent mounds of the medieval tin works at Erme Pits, where there is a bewilderment of tin streamings and large boulders.

Here, on the north side of the Erme valley, the tinners dug out a deep, narrow gully - probably to follow the tin lode - and nowadays its sides provide a home for a large number of rabbits. I always find it astonishing that

Erme Pits.

The 'A' Stone, with the inscription highlighted by some handy Dartmoor 'ooze', and the camera case placed to give an idea of scale!

there should be a thriving colony of rabbits this far out on the high moor, having never seen a single one in the vicinity of any other former warren on Dartmoor. Their presence begs the question of how they came there in the first place. Perhaps one explanation is that they are the descendants of animals that lived in the Crane Hill Warren operated by Reverend William Daykin of Sheepstor for some 20 years from 1867. Crane Hill is 2 miles from Erme Pits, but the warren apparently covered a large area as its boundary was said to have included Nun's Cross, Plym Head, Erme Head and Plym Steps. Whatever their origin, it is always a pleasant surprise to enter this gully to be greeted by the thudding of paws on the firm ground as the rabbits scramble for the safety of the innumerable burrows in the gully sides.

The River Erme trickles out of a stretch of boggy ground beyond Erme Pits, and in order to find its symbolic head, you should now walk over the dry ground to the west of the mire. Look for the 'A' Stone, a long, low boulder situated near the edge of the bog and about 400 metres north of Erme Pits. The stone has the inscription 'A Head' engraved on its southern face, but it is very faint and is best seen when the sun is shining from the south-east or south-west. The 'A' denotes Arme, this being the old name for Erme: it is not known when the inscription was made, but it must be many centuries old. In the 1240 perambulation 'A Head' was a defined point on the Forest boundary and was called Grymsgrove. It is surmised that the name was derived from a grove of upland oak trees, similar to those at Wistman's Wood, that may have been growing here at the time of the 1240 perambulation but were later cut down for fuel and timber by the tinners at Erme Pits.

A walk in the upper Erme valley on a fine day is one of the most sublime experiences to be had on Dartmoor. The understated beauty, the remoteness, the seclusion and the near-certain absence of any other human being all combine to give a powerful sensation of having broken free from the madcap daily routine of modern living to enter a landscape where time stands still.

In contrast to the great solitude and beauty that now prevail at Erme Head, the presence of the tin workings nearby must once have presented a very busy (and unsightly) scene of early industry. But the remains of the workings and the nearby Forest boundary make this a very significant area in the history of Dartmoor. It is a striking experience to stand at Erme Head and contemplate all this while gazing over a landscape of short grass studded with large boulders that stretches away eastwards into the dreamy distance of the upper Erme valley.

[1] I have referred here to chapter 6 of *Dartmoor Forest Farms* by Elisabeth Stanbrook (Devon Books, 1994) for the information on Frederick Symes and the history of Huntingdon Warren House.

[2] For clarity of the map accompanying this chapter, I have not shown the peat and china clay tramways or remains, nor have I shown the Abbots' Way. But no doubt you will be walking with a 1:25,000 scale O.S. map (or if not you should be!) and this shows all these features.

7. Erme Head to Princetown – 4.8 miles

Starting point: The main car park at Princetown.
Grid ref: SX 589 735.
Total length of walk: Around 10 miles.

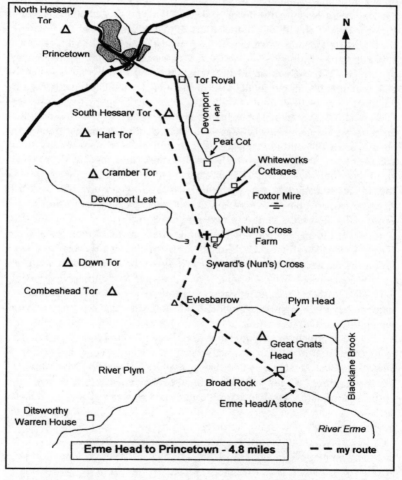

Erme Head to Princetown - 4.8 miles   – – my route

There are several routes out to Erme Head, but my preference, other than going along the Forest boundary in reverse, is to follow the cycle track from Princetown via South Hessary Tor as far as Nun's (Syward's) Cross, then walk up to Hand Hill (SX 609 688), down to Plym Ford and, finally, along the so-called 'Abbots' Way'.

Once you have arrived at Erme Head it is noticeable that the western skyline is very close and, where it dips, it is just possible to discern a wide tract of shorter grass worn by the footsteps of walkers. Make for this across the damp ground around the 'A' Stone and soon you will be on the very lip of the watershed between the Erme and the Plym, passing about 200 metres above a large flat slab of granite inscribed 'BB Broad Rock'. 'BB' denotes Blachford Bounds, the boundary of the manor of Blachford, near Cornwood, although the inscription is now indistinct, especially when lit by the high sun of summer. Broad Rock, incidentally, is not listed as a bound point in the 1240 perambulation, but is included in the modern boundary recognised by the Duchy of Cornwall.

In order to stay on the Forest boundary from Erme Head to the summit of Eylesbarrow, as delineated in 1240, you need to follow a straight-line course on a bearing of approximately 303°. The only defined path nearby is the section of the Abbots' Way which curves around the slope of Great Gnats Head and continues downwards to Plym Ford. However, at this point you should remain above the path and, instead, head directly towards Eylesbarrow. In doing so, you now leave the enchanting seclusion of the Erme valley and see a wide vista opening up before you. To your left - the south - you can see Langcombe Hill, while Hen Tor, Lee Moor, Sheeps Tor, Hartor, Calveslake Tor and Evil Combe are all visible in a westerly direction. From this distance there is no hint of evil about the combe, which appears merely as a distant feature giving some character to the otherwise mainly unbroken sweep of the expansive southern slope of Eylesbarrow. Immediately to the right, the shoulder of Great Gnats Head prevents you from seeing the cairn on its summit.

As you continue, the Plym can be seen disappearing around the shoulder of Eastern Tor, on which a distinctive track and trees reveal the position of Ditsworthy Warren House, while further east the TV mast on North Hessary Tor looms above Crane Hill, marking the direction of Princetown, your ultimate destination. Heather is well established on this hillside, particularly at the point where you cross the Abbots' Way and begin the final drop to the River Plym. Every so often you may find that you are following a narrow path that strays on to your theoretical beeline through the long grass. If so, like me, you may well wonder whether it has been formed from the footsteps of other perambulators, or whether it results merely from the wandering of grazing animals.

Down near the Plym itself you head towards the river through the maze of tin workings on the valley floor. You should be able to cross the river quite easily and haul yourself up the steep bank opposite. There now comes a long, long slog up the southern slope of Eylesbarrow; contrary to its appearance as an even-graded, moderate climb, the lower part of its slope is much steeper than further up. The summit lies just over half a mile from the river.

The route - for don't forget that you are still supposed to be following a notional straight line from Erme Head to the summit of Eylesbarrow - takes you between Evil Combe and the old Crane Hill tin workings, which had later become part of the more recent and much more extensive Eylesbarrow Mine to the west. Everywhere there are mounds of tinners' spoil, many with extensive coverings of bright purple heather in late summer. As abundant are a multiplicity of filled-in shafts, some of which are still quite deep; at the base of these pits you can sometimes find a damp micro-habitat of ferns and mosses thriving in the deepest part, where sunlight never penetrates.

Next, cross the stony track that curves around the side of Eylesbarrow. Then, after 250 metres or so, you will reach the summit of the massive hill and the spot at which a short iron spike, with a head shaped like that of a cobra and carrying the badly-worn inscription 'FB' (Forest Bound), may be found. Unfortunately, it is also around this area that a few passing walkers fulfil an urge to create in stone; sometimes one finds Stonehenge in miniature

Eylesbarrow summit, with Duchy of Cornwall iron 'cobra's head' and Burrator catchment boundstone, denoting the boundary of Plymouth Corporation Waterworks.

or a good replica of the remains of Statts House on northern Dartmoor. It's rather a pity that artistic licence has to manifest itself on such a prominent and historical place on Dartmoor, besides which it is only a matter of time before the original cairn will be wholly altered from its original form.

Having plodded over much rough ground to the top of Eylesbarrow, you will be rewarded with an extensive view over the surrounding few miles of Dartmoor. In clockwise order, as you survey the scene, comes a veritable 'who's who' of Dartmoor landmarks - Cox, Roos, Great Mis, North Hessary and Great Links Tors, Summer Hill, Rough Tor, the Whitehorse Hill/Quinter's Man ridge, Sittaford Tor, Fernworthy Forest, Hameldon, Ter Hill, Ryder's Hill, Great Gnats Head, Langcombe Hill, Hen Tor, Trowlesworthy Tors, Lee Moor, Sheepstor, Lether Tor and Sharp Tor. Away to the south-west, beyond Dartmoor, Plymouth Sound can also be clearly seen.

There can be little doubt that the prominence of Eylesbarrow was the principal reason for its inclusion as a Forest bound in 1240 and thereafter. And, given the very abstract straight line that was pursued by the 1240 boundary from Erme Head, an unambiguous boundary marker was certainly needed at this stage. When I walked from Erme Head to Eylesbarrow I came across no indications whatever of any defined path or other sign to indicate the presence of the line of the Forest boundary. All the established paths and tracks crossed my route at something approaching a right-angle. In fact, the 1608 perambulation had added Plym Head to the list of boundary points, and this created a considerable deviation from the 1240 boundary. The 1608 perambulation may once again have formalised tacitly accepted bounds that had evolved since the first perambulation 368 years previously. Or perhaps the 1608 jurors were surreptitiously trying to reduce the area of the Forest and provide more free grazing on the open moor!

Soon after you leave Eylesbarrow, now following a bearing of about 25°, the Forest boundary suddenly becomes a very real and tangible feature, for ahead it is defined in straight lines on the ground. Numerous boundstones, shaped by the feather and tare method of splitting with metal wedges and inscribed 'PCWW 1917', not only denote the boundary of the catchment area of Burrator Reservoir (purchased in that year by the Plymouth Corporation Waterworks undertaking) but also happen to be located next to the boundary of the Forest itself. The boundary is, in fact, on the line of the prominent path, now serving the second purpose of a cycle track, that heads straight for Nun's Cross and there bends slightly to the west on a course for South Hessary Tor. The path is affected badly by 'poaching' from the feet of grazing animals until you reach the cycle track proper, at which point you have the luxury (for Dartmoor) of walking on a very smooth surface of rolled-in growan, or decomposed granite. This was first laid by the Dartmoor National Park Authority in 1995/96.

I have mixed views about the presence of a cycle track out here on the wild moor. Certainly, if it was used by large numbers of cyclists, it would represent a significant intrusion into the special seclusion and sanctity of the landscape. But even on the August day of my walk I encountered no more than eight cyclists, most of whom appeared to be cycling from Princetown out to no further than Nun's Cross and then returning - scarcely an invasion. What's more, I have to confess that my family and I enjoyed a few hours of cycling here ourselves in August 1999 while staying on the moor to see the total solar eclipse. We hired five bikes from Peek Hill Farm and rode up the bumpy trackbed of the old Yelverton to Princetown railway. We stopped at Princetown to have lunch and some respite from saddle soreness, and then continued out to Eylesbarrow on what was a wonderfully smooth and very interesting ride. It was a novel experience to travel at speed over the moor and in such comfort. The ride from South Hessary Tor to Nun's Cross was positively exhilarating, but was followed by a stiff climb to the top of Eylesbarrow. Then came another downhill swoop, this time to the Scout Hut near Gutter Tor, before taking to the metalled road to Sheepstor, where two of us nearly came a cropper on the sharp downhill bends. A more sedate ride around the edge of Burrator Reservoir and across the dam led us on to Burrator Lodge and so back to Peek Hill Farm. All this took place in bright sunshine (which was notably absent on the morning of the total eclipse!). So the cycle track offers a different Dartmoor experience, albeit one which should not be provided on many (or perhaps any) other parts of the high moor.

When they use the cycle track back to Princetown, few cyclists probably realise that they are following the same route taken by the perambulators in their historic mission of 1240. Aside from the well-defined line of the boundary, there is much else to see as you walk northwards down the slope of Eylesbarrow. For a start, there is Nun's Cross Farm, the isolated house perched on the edge of the great central basin of Dartmoor. The present house (built in 1901) is next to the site of the original and humble single-storey dwelling completed by John Hooper in 1871. One can only wonder at the sheer optimism and pioneering spirit that led him to establish his farm in such an exposed place and eventually make a success of it. Then, beyond the farm, Fox Tor Mire can be seen stretching away into the distance to the narrow gap between the lower slopes of Ter Hill and Royal Hill, through which the River Swincombe flows. Dominating the middle distance is North Hessary Tor and its television mast, while nearer to hand is South Hessary Tor. Beyond them loom the hills of northern Dartmoor, on the far side of the central basin.

Leaving the northern slope of Eylesbarrow, you will come to Nun's Cross. In my view, this ancient stone object - standing over 7 feet high - is the most evocative of all the boundary points on the 1240 perambulation. True, the natural markers of the boundary, such as Great Mis Tor and Cosdon Hill, are outstanding and permanent landmarks. But how miraculous it is that a

The impressive Nun's, or Syward's, Cross, with the farm in
the background.

relatively small and vulnerable man-made structure should have survived in
place for more than 750 years since the first perambulation of the Forest. Not
that the role of Forest bound was its original purpose - it is believed to have
been erected up to 50 years or so prior to the 1240 perambulation. The fact
that it is a symbol of the Christian faith points to a religious origin, perhaps
in forming a marker along a route over the high moor between the abbeys of
Tavistock and Buckfast (the other crosses marking the route being, from west
to east, Newleycombe Cross, Goldsmith's Cross, Childe's Tomb, Mount
Misery Cross, the two crosses on Ter Hill, Skir Ford Cross, Horse Ford Cross
and Horn's Cross). On its eastern face the inscription 'Syward' can be made

out; this is almost certainly a reference to Syward, Earl of Northumberland, who owned nearby land in the reign of Edward the Confessor. On the western face of the cross is an inscribed cross, beneath which are the words 'Boc Lond', believed to denote the lands of Buckland Abbey situated to the west. A more general meaning might be 'book land' - or land held by charter.

Although the cross is sometimes referred to as Syward's Cross, it is more commonly known as Nun's Cross. According to William Crossing this was derived from the Celtic *nans* - a valley, dale or ravine - and of course the location of the cross would warrant such a name. It must have been an easy decision for the twelve jurors to choose Nun's Cross as a boundary marker of the Forest, given its prominence. Another point of interest is that in 1846 the stem of the cross was broken when it was pushed over by two boys out searching for cattle; the iron strap used to make the repair is still in place.

Nun's Cross is located in an area that encapsulates so many of Dartmoor's historical and cultural themes. Aside from the cross itself and the Forest boundary, there is the Devonport Leat, by which water was ingeniously conducted to Plymouth, using gravity alone, to supply the dockyards there at the end of the 18th century. Underneath one's feet is the Devonport Leat Tunnel, which takes this watercourse under the Swincombe-Meavy watershed, impassable by any other means. The tunnel symbolises the determination and ability of those who lived during the Industrial Revolution to create ambitious works of engineering for the greater good of the population at large. Then there is the simple heroism of John Hooper who, in the 1870s, established and succeeded in creating a working farm in this exposed and often rainswept area. Finally, there is the brooding presence nearby of Fox Tor Mire, the Great Grimpen Mire in Conan Doyle's *The Hound of the Baskervilles*, in which Nun's Cross Farm itself may well have inspired the fictitious 'Merripit House'.

Beyond Nun's Cross you should continue along the dusty white track towards Princetown. Initially, this involves going uphill but, once you have reached the top of the first slope, the path levels out somewhat and stretches away from you, bullet straight, into the far distance where South Hessary Tor sits on the skyline. Indeed, at this point the tor is still over a mile away and it is only after what seems like an age that you finally reach it; on the southern approach it is noticeable that the track is not on the true boundary line, which is, in fact, marked by a boundstone some 20 metres out in the grassland to the east.

South Hessary Tor (known locally as Lookout Tor and as 'Ysfother' in the description of the 1240 perambulation) is a typical medium-sized Dartmoor tor, apart from the presence, on its summit, of another iron 'cobra's head' Forest bound marker identical to that on Eylesbarrow. From the top of the tor there is a tremendous view, with North Hessary Tor ('another Ysfother' in 1240) and its television mast dominating the skyline to the north.

South Hessary Tor, with Duchy of Cornwall iron 'cobra's head' prominent.

The view north from South Hessary Tor along the 1240 boundary to North Hessary Tor.

The Forest boundary line deviates by a few degrees to the west immediately north of South Hessary Tor and it is again remarkable how closely the boundstones line up between here and the rocks (not the mast!) of North Hessary Tor. So, true to your task, leave the tor not by the path, but by following the line of boundstones towards North Hessary Tor, which, given its height, must almost have nominated itself to the jurors as their next boundary point. After a walk of about half a mile that takes you through long grass past the PCWW and other boundstones (one PCWW stone curiously being roughly cut in marked contrast to the others, which are more geometric) you will then arrive at the top of a ridge looking out over Princetown.

The view over this remarkable Dartmoor settlement emphasises the exposed solitude of its position, with an unyielding backcloth of Great Mis Tor and the other heights of northern Dartmoor. The high-chimneyed monoliths of Dartmoor Prison add a dimension of classic grimness to the scene. Beneath you is the legacy of Sir Thomas Tyrwhitt, another Dartmoor pioneer who, in the early 1800s, built the prison and a small town to support it, but whose grandiose plans to enclose the moor for agriculture fortunately came to nothing, thwarted by the Dartmoor climate. Above all this there now looms the modern monstrosity of the television mast.

All these developments, of course, came centuries after Henry III sent his jurors on their task to fix the Forest boundary. To them, the site of what is now Princetown was then no more than a plateau at the head of the River Meavy; they would have hurried past and on to the summit of North Hessary Tor without a second glance. It is probably a safe bet that it was also raining at the time!

A short walk down Plymouth Hill brings you to the main car park by the visitor centre. You can then rest your aching legs and look forward to the next stage of your personal perambulation, particularly as it will lead you towards the wilds of the northern moor - never a place to be taken lightly.

—8. Princetown to Great Mis Tor – 2.7 miles —

Starting point: The main car park at Princetown.
Grid ref: SX 589 735.
Other important information: Walk lies partly (ie the area around Great Mis Tor) within the Merrivale Firing Range.
Total length of walk: Around 5¹/₂ miles.

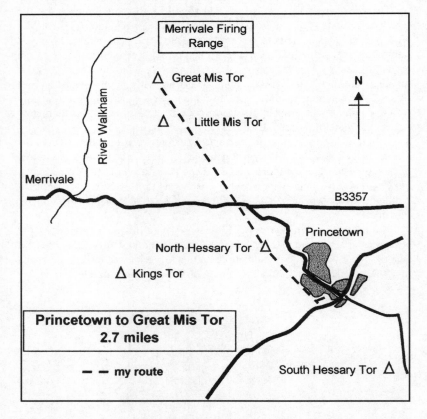

Set off through the car park exit, turn left into the road that once led to Princetown railway station, then branch off to the right along a footpath across some open ground, through a five-bar gate, and head for North Hessary Tor. Along the way you will pass some new houses on your right - and then the climb begins! In ascending the dome-like profile of North Hessary Tor, you will soon have a panoramic view if you look back over Princetown, but your attention will revert constantly to the massive galvanised steel tower of the North Hessary Tor television mast that rears into the sky ahead of you.

The mast is, of course, wholly out of place on the moor. It was erected in 1953, as if in early rebuttal of the notion that the landscape of national parks (of which Dartmoor had become one, two years previously) would be free of this sort of blemish. Seen from far off, the mast gives a reminder of the direction of Princetown, provided that at least part of it is visible beneath any canopy of cloud that prevails on the day. A series of red lights, very prominent on a gloomy day and at night, flashes on and off along its height to warn low-flying aircraft of its presence. When you reach the hilltop you realise just how huge it is; three single cables run from the very top to the ground, while, from part-way up its height, paired cables provide further support. The cable stays themselves are fixed to the ground by holding-down bolts secured to massive concrete anchorages. An unmemorable, but functional, blockhouse sits near the base of the mast, with its own narrow metalled access road.

The mast dwarfs the admittedly rather modest rock-pile of North Hessary Tor itself. But it is worth reminding yourself that the Forest boundary was

North Hessary Tor (with cables and anchorage for the TV mast).

here 713 years before the mast was erected, and it is the rocks of the tor that form the boundary point. Try to ignore the presence of the mast and clamber carefully up to the triangulation point on the tor to take in the tremendous view that is on offer. To the south-east, the shoulder of the hill hides Princetown, but South Hessary Tor stands out, as does the line of boundary stones linking it to this point. In the other direction lies the stark outline of Great Mis Tor, its huge slopes crowned by a jagged outcrop of granite. Again, notice how the enclosure boundary lies exactly on the line between the two summits that forms the Forest boundary.

The view to Great Mis Tor from North Hessary Tor.

Now move off down the hill to the next landmark, the anvil-like Rundlestone Tor. From here, there is a good view over a nice little pastoral scene immediately below, comprising a set of four small fields enclosed by drystone walls and invariably occupied by a large flock of sheep or a few inquisitive grazing cattle. There is a footpath through these fields on the Forest boundary line with good solid stiles over the walls and you must take this path if you are to follow a purist route exactly along the boundary! Alternatively, if you are deterred by the presence of bulky beasts, then you can stay on the open moor by walking round the western edge of the walled enclosure.

After you cross the stile that gives access to the main road it is worth taking care on the other side - one trip or slip and you will finish up on the busy highway quicker than anticipated! Nearby you will notice something that is fast becoming a historical relic - a red telephone box. It would be perfectly understandable if British Telecom had decided that the newer type, with a gap between the ground and the sides, might be rather too well ventilated to be used up here at Rundlestone! Whatever, it would be nice to think that some of the old boxes can remain in use rather than being swept away into memory.

Now cross the road and follow a track signposted 'Footpath to the Moor' - something of an understatement you might think, the track actually being of far greater significance than most. Soon you come across the remains of a stone building filled with a depressing mass of rusting fence wire, after which a degree of care may be needed; if there has been heavy rain recently the track is liable to have become an impromptu stream formed by excess run-off from the nearby hillside to the north. Nevertheless, it is still walkable, and before long you are passing another stone building, this time with a corrugated iron roof but with its southern wall leaning precariously on two large stone gateposts acting as makeshift flying buttresses.

From hereon the climb up the slope of Great Mis Tor becomes more rapid, and for the major part there is a boundary wall topped by a wire fence on your right. This is the western wall of the New Forest Enclosure. Every so often you also encounter a marker stone that does not have any inscription to reveal its purpose, but is plainly intended to denote the boundary between the Forest and Walkhampton Parish. Just like the section south of Princetown, the Forest boundary here is clearly defined on the ground.

On arriving at Great Mis Tor you will have reached one of the most prominent boundary markers on the entire perambulation. Back in 1240 the twelve jurors sent by Henry III would have found the boundary quite easy to delineate over the previous few miles from Eylesbarrow to South and North Hessary tors and on to Great Mis Tor. Now, as they looked northwards over the empty moorland, they would have seen a number of other distant high points, such as Hare Tor and Great Links Tor. But as we will see, they chose neither of these points and instead picked their way in a subtle manner across ridges and up river valleys using, most probably, local guides to help them in areas where there were no obvious candidates for boundary points.

There was no ambiguity about the status of Great Mis Tor, though. This is a great tor of Dartmoor, both in terms of its prominence to the distant observer and of the view to be had from the summit. On a clear day you can see right down to Plymouth in the south, while northwards, Fur Tor, Cut Hill, Great Kneeset, High Willhays, Great Links Tor and Hare Tor will be clearly visible. On one rockpile of Great Mis Tor itself is a large rock basin known as Mistor Pan, first noted centuries ago and formed by the effects of freezing and thawing of water over millions of years.

I was once caught up here in heavy rain and, having half-expected it, had packed a small foldaway umbrella, not a widely used item of macho walking equipment, I have to confess. But I didn't see why I shouldn't be well equipped to keep dry, having endured many previous windswept drenchings on Great Mis Tor. As the heavens opened, on went my leggings, out came the umbrella and, with the rain at my back, I set off back down the slope towards Princetown feeling very comfortable and very dry. As I approached the northern boundary wall of the New Forest Enclosure, I saw some walkers coming towards me. I could see that they were soaking wet, walking face into the wind. I was contemplating how not to look self-conscious under my umbrella when my mobile phone rang. This was a godsend, because it enabled me to walk past this group of walkers, concentrating on my phone call without having to look them in the eye!

Retrace your steps to the main road, over North Hessary Tor and on to Princetown. Beyond the latter you can see the straight line of Castle Road leading out to Tor Royal. This farm, built and occupied by Sir Thomas Tyrwhitt, symbolises the order that he sought to impose on Dartmoor.

This short stage of the Forest boundary has taken you to Great Mis Tor and to the end of the convenient straight lines defining the boundary on the ground. Beyond this point all sight of civilisation is left behind and you will find yourself navigating through an altogether wilder landscape.

9. Great Mis Tor to Limsboro Cairn – 2.4 miles

Starting point: The Four Winds car park, between Merrivale and Two Bridges.
Grid ref: SX 561 749.
Other important information: North of Great Mis Tor the walk lies within the Merrivale Firing Range.
Total length of walk: Around 7 miles.

Set off up the stony military track opposite Four Winds car park that leads towards Little and Great Mis tors. The walk to these tors is deceptively further than it looks when you start and will take longer than anticipated.

On the day I walked the first part of this route, I had an unforgettable reminder of the cruel ways of nature. A strange cry behind me caused me to turn round, and I was just in time to see two peregrine falcons striking at a hapless pigeon which, having taken a wicked strike from sharp talons, plummeted to the ground as if it had been shot. One of the falcons followed the victim down, while the other flew away. As they did so, I saw a flock of racing pigeons flying around in a very disturbed way; clearly it had been one of their number that had been felled by the peregrines. It appeared that the falcon following the pigeon down was an immature bird learning to hunt and kill. Anyway, after a short time, it flew away as well, uttering the same strange cry that had first attracted my attention. I then walked back 200 metres down the hill and found the pigeon, bleeding from a talon wound but still alive. It had bright yellow legs, each bearing a prominent ring. I should probably have despatched it with my boot, but decided to let nature take its course, not knowing if the peregrine would decline to eat a bird that it had not killed itself.

As I walked back up the hill there was no sign of the peregrines, so I decided that I would check the pigeon on the return leg of the walk and then despatch it if it was still alive. I need not have bothered; later, when I did return, all that was left was a pile of bloodied feathers.

To return to your own walk, head up the slope past Little Mis Tor and eventually you will reach the majestic rock stacks of Great Mis Tor itself. Having perhaps rested here and admired the extensive views, you should now continue past two military look-out huts, which are painted in a dark camouflage pattern. A fairly steep drop then brings you out on to the more level ground of Mistor Marsh; keeping to the left (west) of centre of this plateau, you will find that the ground is fairly firm in most places and you should be able to make good progress, soon reaching the edge of the narrow valley carved out by the River Walkham.

I always find this a particularly entrancing place. As one approaches the Walkham there is a sudden change from exposed high ground to the sheltered seclusion of a young river valley. Thousands of years ago early man must have felt the same, because there are a number of hut circles on the northern

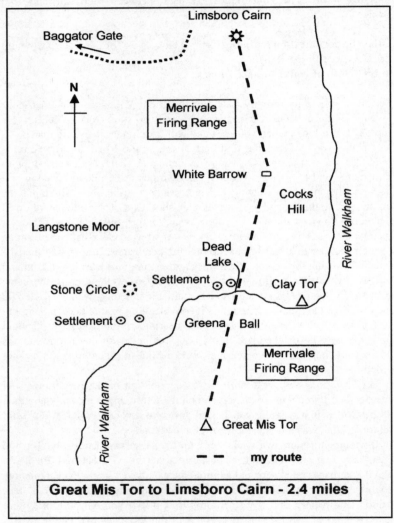

Great Mis Tor to Limsboro Cairn - 2.4 miles

side of the Walkham. These huts were built in a location that was low enough to be sheltered, but far enough up the north side of the valley to catch some sunshine for most of the year. There would have been a plentiful supply of water and, no doubt in those days, digestive systems were more hardened to the bacteria that flourish in it! Grazing for animals was also in limitless supply. The passing jurors might well have looked at the hut circles and felt how much more civilised the human race had become compared to those primitive days. In turn, we ourselves look back on the era of the first perambulation with the same very distant perspective.

Make for the small stream known as Dead Lake, which runs through ancient tin streamings on the north side of the Walkham valley. Not that Dead Lake was mentioned in the records of the 1240 Perambulation; but the line from Great Mis Tor to the next 1240 bound - White Barrow - passes very close to it and indeed Dead Lake was listed as a Forest bound in the perambulation of 1608.

It is easier to walk up the western side of Dead Lake than in the long grass and soft ground on the eastern side. Now follow a bearing of 23° over the gradual brow and on to the plateau north of the Walkham valley. Keeping an eye on the compass, you should aim to reach the somewhat nondescript hump of White Barrow. When you arrive there you may wonder, as I did, whether the 1240 perambulators had used White Barrow somewhat reluctantly as a

White Barrow, with backpack giving some idea of the scale of this difficult-to-photograph subject.

Limsboro Cairn, with the military flagpole.

boundary marker, and only because there was no better option. Nevertheless, White Barrow did have one factor in its favour as a bound point - it lies immediately next to the ancient Lich Path, which is well defined across this otherwise rather featureless area.

From White Barrow the Forest boundary continues in a straight line to Limsboro Cairn, on a bearing of 350°. You should, in fact, now be able to see its rock stump, if the conditions are clear, away in front of you up a long, gradual slope. As you leave the Lich Path behind, the ground falls away on your left to give a dramatic view westwards to the distant hills of Cornwall. This fine panorama is similar to the view to be had from most parts of western Dartmoor - the lower ground of the Tamar valley backed by a blue-grey line of hills, principally those of Bodmin Moor.

The high ridge leading to Limsboro gives the walker the sensation of being partly surrounded by the major Dartmoor peaks; behind lie Great Mis Tor, the Staple Tors and Roos Tor, while to the north are Great Links Tor, Amicombe Hill, High Willhays, Great Kneeset, Fur Tor and Cut Hill. The sombre prospect of those lonely heights would have concentrated the thoughts of the 1240 perambulators as they made their way northwards. They would have been aware that their task was by now well advanced, but with some tricky decisions still to be made. The line they selected in this area placed the Forest boundary very close to the edge of the high moor, with cultivated ground clearly visible at the foot of the slope.

Nearer to hand, as you approach Limsboro Cairn and the end of your walk, you will notice the shallow cut of the southern section of Black Lane, a track that once gave access from Baggator Gate to peat workings at Walkham Head. Then finally, on reaching the cairn, you have a good opportunity for another rest, perhaps taking advantage of the rocks to shelter from the wind for a while. On my last visit I noticed that there was now a solar panel on the military flagpole here, no doubt to aid the charging of batteries for radios and field telephones.

The simplest way of returning to the starting point is to retrace your steps. Otherwise a more easterly route back to the car will take in much wetter and more awkward ground on the north-eastern side of Great Mis Tor, while a more westerly route will include the Walkham valley and a long trek up the hill from Merrivale to Four Winds.

This relatively short section of the Forest boundary provides a fine walk and some dramatic scenery which is probably no less impressive than that presented to the twelve jurors on that June day more than 760 years ago.

10. Limsboro Cairn to Rattlebrook Head – 4.5 miles

Starting point: Just inside Baggator Gate, off the track.
Grid ref: SX 547 805.
Other important information: Walk passes through the Merrivale, Willsworthy and Okehampton firing ranges.
Total length of walk: Around 12 miles. I have included an alternative route for the return journey.

The ideal parking place for the next stage of the perambulation is Baggator Gate, on the western side of Dartmoor. After leaving the A386 at Mary Tavy, you will need to drive along a series of convoluted lanes that takes you through Horndon, past the Elephant's Nest pub, then through Hilltown, over Hill Bridge, past Wapsworthy and finally on to the moor at Baggator Gate, where there is space for a few cars to park just inside, off the track.

Set off along the stony track that leads from Baggator Gate towards the open moor. You will soon come to a military look-out hut and should then pass through a gate on to the open moor. Immediately beyond the gate is a 'stroll' that funnels outwards towards the high ridge on which are located Limsboro Cairn and Lynch Tor. The track, meanwhile, becomes a shallow, sunken indentation on a closely-grazed slope.

Soon the walls on either side swing abruptly away from each other, while the track itself, actually part of Black Lane, curves a little more gradually around to the north. But your route lies almost due east, directly up the ridge towards the Limsboro military flagpole. As you climb, the grassy slope becomes more studded with rocks, and your pulse will pound in your ears in protest at such prolonged and prolific use of energy! Eventually, though, you reach Limsboro Cairn, its flagless pole pointing skywards. Nearby is the gargoyle of Lynch Tor which, from the right direction, looks like a large-nosed individual wearing a flat cap.

From this ridge you are treated to a fabulous view extending to the distant heights of the northern moor. But the first destination on your walk, Rattlebrook Foot, where the Rattlebrook joins the River Tavy, is actually hidden below the high ground of Standon Down. However, a glance at the map shows you that the direct route to Rattlebrook Foot almost lines up with Great Links Tor - a very prominent landmark. Before you depart from Limsboro in that direction, look behind you and note how the 1240 perambulators would have been able to see back along their route to Great Mis Tor, some 2¹/₂ miles to the south.

Unfortunately, soon after setting off, you will almost certainly run into some of the usual difficulties faced by anyone trying to walk in straight lines on Dartmoor - wet and rough ground. Indeed, you may have to abandon a

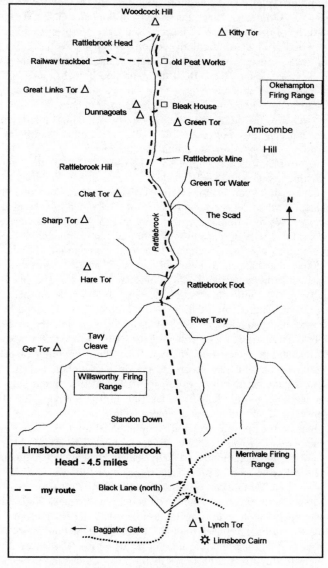

Reproduced by permission of Ordnance Survey on behalf of The Controller of Her Majesty's Stationery Office, © Crown Copyright 100042123.

rigid straight line to avoid the softer areas as you drop down the slope towards the sunken track of Black Lane. This is quite steep-sided itself in places, and I recall finding a pipit's nest containing four eggs tucked into the bank here a few years ago. Originally, Black Lane led from Baggator Gate over the open moor to turf-ties near the head of Eastern Red Lake. From this main track, a branch curved around the northern end of the Limsboro-Lynch Tor ridge, doubling back on itself before turning east over the River Walkham to more peat-ties near Walkham Head. Both the main and branch tracks are useful ways of crossing what is otherwise very awkward ground, the former giving a good start to a walk to Fur Tor and the latter to Walkham Head.

Your route now lies across Standon Down which, again, is often rather wet in places, but generally not too bad to walk over. Rather than being a flat plateau, Standon Down does have some undulations and is much wider than you expect; in fact, it is very similar to Nakers Hill on the southern moor. Its lack of distinct features, however, made it a very unsuitable area on which to define such an important feature as the Forest boundary. Consequently, it is understandable why the later perambulators of 1608 opted for a boundary line that followed Western Redlake to the Tavy and then turned downstream to Rattlebrook Foot, in preference to a straight line across Standon Down. Such re-definition may also have been an example of the continual nibbling away at the Forest that happened down the centuries as commoners sought to extend their grazing areas into the high moorland owned by the Duchy.

A rather tiring 2-mile slog eventually brings you to the northern end of Standon Down. Approaching the Tavy, the initially gradual slope becomes much steeper and you are confronted by a fine view of Rattlebrook Foot. To your right is the narrow, rocky valley of the Tavy, with Fur Tor beyond. To the left, in autumn at any rate, there will be some mingling of beautiful brown, olive green and light green colours of the vegetation at the foot of Hare Tor. Up the Rattlebrook valley itself, Green Tor stands out on the northern skyline, its normally nondescript profile perhaps given extra prominence by a splash of cloud shadow. Only the two cubical military lookout huts on the opposite slope of Amicombe Hill mar the view.

When I came this way I once more found myself trying to get into the minds of the 1240 perambulators. Why had they chosen a boundary that followed the Rattlebrook in preference to one that followed the ridge from Hare Tor to Chat Tor and on to Great Links Tor? Was it because (as I have speculated earlier in this book) they had been briefed to leave some common land for the population to use, or because they had decided to make use of both streams and lines between high points to define the boundary? There is no clear answer, but one thing to be said for using the Rattlebrook is that it was a linear feature that ran in the northerly direction that the perambulators wished to follow. It is also significant that, on reaching Rattlebrook Head, their chosen line began to turn clockwise towards their starting point at

Rattlebrook Foot, with the Tavy in the foreground.

Cosdon. So the brook could have been chosen for its close fit to the natural shape of the boundary that would be needed.

From your elevated perch at the northern end of Standon Down you now have to drop down into the Tavy valley. To your left (the west) the slope becomes steeper still and it is advisable to clamber slowly down to the right among boulders which, shaded from direct sunlight for much of the year, have become encrusted with a thick coating of moss. Once on the valley floor, you will have to search for suitable stepping stones in the bifurcated river to cross to the northern bank. Then make your way towards the Rattlebrook confluence, which should now be on your left, and follow the brook upstream for some metres before stepping carefully over more rocks to its western bank.

At its lower end, the valley of the Rattlebrook is narrow and steep-sided, with little room for easy walking in some places. It is also quite boggy, awkward and tiring. However, your attention will be diverted by the interesting, and massive, earthworks of the former Cur Beam tin working on the left until you reach the point where the valley begins to widen and the brook itself meanders across a more level valley floor. Henceforth, the going gradually becomes easier; a firm track leads over short-grazed grass which contrasts with the longer- and probably very wet - grass now being left behind.

You can now also see much further up the valley and appreciate what a secluded place it is. To the west, the bulk of Rattlebrook Hill is very close at hand, while on the right is the gargantuan Amicombe Hill, its western face carved into a huge tilted basin that gives birth to the two streamlets known as Green Tor Water and The Scad. On the valley floor are innumerable heather-clad tin-streaming mounds, and in the distance the valley floor itself becomes much steeper and rises to meet the skyline in a narrow 'V', framed on one side by Higher Dunnagoat and on the other by Green Tor. Between these two the ruins of Bleak House point forlornly to the sky.

As you approach the northern end of the level valley floor, the path begins to climb among the ruins of the former Rattlebrook Mine; here the heather cannot conceal the extensive area of workings and ruined structures. On the opposite bank, a deep girt is gouged into the slope of Amicombe Hill. Next, you walk past the point where the access track to the mine comes in from High Down, by The Dartmoor Inn, and then the valley quickly diminishes into a narrow, v-shaped gully in which the infant Rattlebrook tumbles down from above. This part of the stream-bed was probably deepened by the tin miners to drain what may once have been a tarn and is now a flat, miry area above Bleak House.

The last time I was here, Bleak House itself had lost still more of its structure to the elements. Once occupied by the manager of the Rattlebrook Peat Works, a quarter of a mile to the north, it is now a forlorn ruin whose prime use is as a shelter for sheep or people caught in the teeth of a storm. It is built in as sheltered a spot as is likely to be found up here, sandwiched between the Dunnagoat Tors and Green Tor in the narrow cleft of the valley of the

The Rattlebrook flows through a channel probably deepened by the tinners.

Rattlebrook. Its name sums up the nature of its location; while there are many places on Dartmoor where it would be quite pleasant to live in good weather, I always sense gloom and foreboding hanging over this part of the moor. All around are the reminders of failed human enterprise - the ruins of Bleak House and the peat works buildings, along with the overgrown geometric regularity of the peat-ties on the nearby slope. Yet its air of desolation makes this a powerful landscape that leaves a deep impression on anyone visiting it.

None of these thoughts would have troubled the perambulators of 1240 as they rode up through this secluded valley. They may have paused to survey with some satisfaction the extent of the task they had already accomplished, for, looking behind them, they would, assuming it was a clear day, have been able to see back along their chosen boundary as far south as North Hessary Tor, some 9 miles distant.

Now make your way along the east side of the valley towards Rattlebrook Peat Works. The ground is extremely soft, with some well-hidden wet patches, and you will probably have to divert up on to the slope to avoid pools of blackened water; in places there are exposed cuts of peat remaining from when the ground was washed away by erosion. In all likelihood there will not be a sound to be heard or another person to be seen when you visit this isolated valley head, and instead the only indication of present-day human activity will be two experimental fenced-off areas, each around eight feet square, which have been created to allow growth to proceed undisturbed by grazing. Not that you would expect much grazing to take place in that wet ground.

Ahead, you will now see Hunt Tor - a little-visited but quite impressive tor in rather featureless surroundings. It is surprising that it was not chosen as a boundary point in preference to the ill-defined head of the Rattlebrook, which lies somewhere up on the funnel-shaped slope to the east of the tor.

Next you come to the site of the Rattlebrook Peat Works buildings, where only the very bases of the walls survive, along with a steel joist projecting aimlessly at the sky. One of the last people to attempt to make the site pay was the writer Thomas Firbank, whose most well-known work was *I Bought*

Hunt Tor, below Rattlebrook Head.

a Mountain (Harrap, 1940). After service in World War II he moved with his family to Southill, near Teigncombe. They lived in a wooden house that he called Shallows, but was known to the locals as Log Hut. This name was, in fact, the title of a book (Harrap, 1954) that he wrote subsequently about his experiences there. The book includes a chapter about his efforts to restart production at Rattlebrook Peat Works and to make it profitable; apparently, while he managed to find an outlet for the peat, the need for expensive mechanisation and the loss of a drying shed to a gale sealed the fate of his enterprise. The works had, in fact, originally been opened in the 1860s and was served by a railway that wound its way up from the London & South Western Railway at Bridestowe. The Royal Marines blew up the works buildings in 1961 - an unfortunate, but typical, instance of the short-sighted demolition of old Dartmoor buildings that has occurred all too frequently since around the 1950s, resulting in the irreplaceable loss of valuable historical structures. It should always be remembered that history does not end 30 years before the present day, but is continuous.

Carry on past the peat works, keeping east of the Rattlebrook. Behind you are Great Links Tor and the causeway of the peat railway. Work your way across to the depression carved out by the Rattlebrook at its head. At one point a track (more prominent on the map than it is on the ground) makes its way over from Hunt Tor and crosses the infant Rattlebrook before heading on towards Kitty Tor. This is as good a place as any to terminate this stage of the perambulation and to return to the starting point.

Before setting off homewards, however, you now have the choice of retracing your steps or taking an alternative route. If you decide on the latter I would recommend that you set off eastwards along the track from Hunt Tor, which becomes sunken into the hillside as it winds its way up on to the Amicombe ridge. Pass Kitty Tor, with its small rock-pile and observation huts, and then head due south along Amicombe Hill. Here, you may spot a military field telephone point with a nearby stone engraved with the number 639, but if not you will certainly enjoy the grandstand view of Fur Tor, Great Kneeset and the lonely centre of northern Dartmoor from this vast ridge. Be warned, though, that the going is rather rough and wet for most of the way as you carry on along the backbone of Amicombe Hill, and it will probably take you a good hour to reach the southern end.

Cross the Tavy at Sandy Ford and head upstream, turning up the valley of Eastern Red Lake. Follow the stream to its head, passing Fuge's Ring Post - a piece of angle iron fixed into a rock, with a ring through a hole in the top. This served as a tethering point for a horse and was installed by Reg Fuge, who occupied Brousentor Farm near Baggator until 1954. Nearby you will find Black Lane and you should then follow it all the way back to the car park at Baggator Gate.

Like me, you will find that the Rattlebrook section of the 1240 Forest boundary is the most secluded part on the northern moor. It engenders a sense of isolation that compares with the stretches from Western Wellabrook to the River Avon and from Red Lake Foot to Erme Head on the southern moor. The walker who ventures out to these places will find, more often than not, that there is no-one else to be seen and that, aside perhaps from the wind rustling the long grass, the silence is total, inspiring a sense that one is intruding on a very special place.

Whether the 1240 perambulators felt privileged to be travelling through such country and felt so inspired, we will never know. Perhaps they merely saw it as part of a job to be done, albeit an important one that had been the subject of a writ issued by the king himself. Whatever their thoughts, they would have known, as they emerged from the valley of the Rattlebrook and continued on to the high ground of Amicombe Hill, that their long journey was now entering its final stages.

— 11. Rattlebrook Head to Yes Tor– 2.2 miles —

Starting point: Meldon Reservoir car park.
Grid ref: SX 563 917.
Other important information: Walk lies partly within the Okehampton Firing Range.
Total length of walk: Around 12 miles.

This section of the perambulation is a very long 2.2 miles! This is because of the necessarily slow and careful descent into the West Okement valley and the steep climb from there to Yes Tor.

My suggested parking place, at Meldon Reservoir, gives a somewhat lengthy route to the starting point at Rattlebrook Head. If desired, a shorter route could be followed from Sourton village via the Rattlebrook Peat Railway trackbed. However, from Meldon, leave the car park and head up on to South Down. Take the path alongside a stone wall and a row of beech trees, which converges gradually among gorse bushes on to the ancient King Way. This track once ran from Okehampton to Tavistock, initially over the high moor - reaching maximum elevation above sea level at Sourton Common - before descending off the moor via the western flank of Great Nodden.

In winter the King Way can be muddy, but is usually passable and quite soon you will emerge on to the open moor south-east of Prewley water treatment works (where water from Meldon Reservoir is treated). Ahead looms a fairly long, stiff climb on to the col between Corn Ridge to the east and the Sourton Tors to the west. This is a strange area in many ways; the turf is so short and uniform that it could pass for a golf course fairway, the resemblance made the more incongruous by the stark pinnacles of the Sourton Tors and, below them, the terracing of the old ice works on Sourton Common.

The ice works was a heroic industrial failure (of which there are many examples on Dartmoor). The idea was that rainwater collecting in a series of terraced basins would freeze in very cold weather and thereby provide a useful supply of ice to the fishermen of Plymouth. Even in the harsher winters of the late 19th century, however, the works quickly proved to be non-viable, but the substantial terracing is plain for all to see to this day; in winter the sun casts long shadows that pick out the terracing prominently. Owing to the profile of the ground, the ice works is seen (and photographed) at its best from a few hundred metres to the east, with the sun in the south or south-east.

The route now takes you to the point where an ancient boundary ditch comes up from Corn Hole and over Sourton Common, crossing the King Way at a scissors-like angle. Close to the intersection is an enigmatic industrial remnant - one half of a large granite apple-crusher. Judging by the careful shaping that had already taken place, the unknown craftsman, nearing the end of his task, apparently took a rather over-ambitious swing with the hammer that proved to be the undoing, or rather splitting, of his giant creation. The other half has disappeared, but the remaining half sits in its place as a monument to the patience (which in this case was tested to the full) of the old craftsman. The complete stone would have been a massive industrial

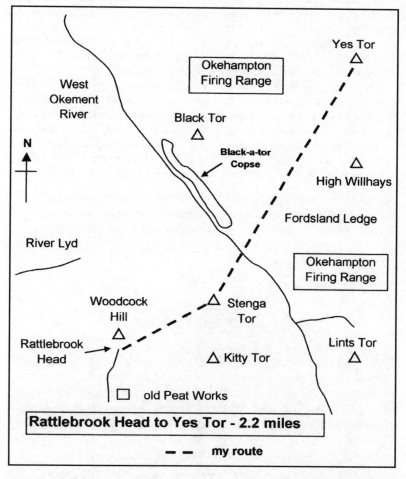

Rattlebrook Head to Yes Tor - 2.2 miles

– – my route

component and one cannot help wondering at the scale of the apple-crushing operation that was contemplated, presumably for use in cider making.

Now follow the lower of two faint tracks on the western slope of Corn Ridge, this track being, in fact, the continuation of the King Way. Winding over a shoulder of hillside, you come to a place known as 'Points', a one-time reversing point on the Rattlebrook Peat Railway. The very firm, stony trackbed now leads southwards, with the silhouette of Great Links Tor dominating the skyline ahead.

As soon as you have crossed the River Lyd leave the railway trackbed for the soft ground over which a path deviates on the east side. This path provides something of a short cut, for it leads past Gren Tor and on over Woodcock Hill to Hunt Tor. Then a short walk of some 200 metres to the east of Hunt Tor finally brings you, after 3½ miles in all, to Rattlebrook Head. This is just the starting point of the next leg of your perambulation!

The exact location of Rattlebrook Head is open to interpretation. There is quite a wide, water-eroded basin that gradually merges into the bulk of Woodcock Hill, but any precision about the head of the brook is, nevertheless, impossible. However, it can be safely assumed that you are at least very close to the right place and that a bearing of 58° will lead you over the gradual brow of the hill towards your next goal, Stenga Tor. This, in turn, means that you will now have to wade away from the Rattlebrook Head area through long

Stenga Tor, with Black Tor beyond.

82

grass and over terrain where the going underfoot is a typical Dartmoor medley of firmness and sogginess. Eventually, though, the ground begins to tilt downwards towards the West Okement valley and you will see the solitary, squat stump of Stenga Tor just a short distance ahead of you, dwarfed by the backdrop of the massive ridge of High Willhays and Yes Tor on the opposite side of the valley.

Stenga Tor is a curious place. As Dartmoor tors go, it would be a complete nonentity were it not for the fact that it is one of the very few rock outcrops on the great 4-mile long Corn Ridge-Amicombe whaleback hill. It is also all that exists of a much larger tor almost totally destroyed by the elements and whose remains now lie littered down the side of the West Okement valley. Similar to Chat Tor on Rattlebrook Hill, Stenga Tor is a miniature, but classic, example of a Dartmoor tor with pseudo-jointing, the familiar serrated profile and a gently curved top.

The 1240 perambulators must have chosen this rather insignificant tor (surrounded by ground that, although sloping, is extremely boggy) as a Forest bound purely because it happened to be located on the general line between Rattlebrook Head and Yes Tor - it could not have been because of its prominence in its own right. They named it La Westsolle, a name evocative of the Norman origins of the twelve jurors.

Contemplating the next stage of the perambulation, from Stenga Tor to Yes Tor, one has to ask whether the 1240 perambulators actually rode their horses along the line of the boundary, as this side of the West Okement valley is very steep and covered in treacherous clitter. It is probably more likely that they dismounted and walked down the valley or simply skirted around the steep section. However they made their onward journey, it would have been remiss of them not to pause, as you should, to admire a remarkable view of the valley. On the opposite side, in winter, the upper part of the High Willhays-Yes Tor ridge is capped with variegated browns; lower down, the slopes are peppered with grey clitter sprinkled over dark brown patches of dead bracken. To the north, the diminutive oak trees of Black-a-Tor Copse spread themselves in an extended, haphazard strip along the slope beneath Black Tor. South of the tor, any sunshine will light up the deep green of the moss-clad clitter directly below you, while further away the folds and erosions of Lints Tor are picked out in subtle shadow. Across this scene meander the lazy blue waters of the West Okement River.

Carry on, making your way past a red and white pole marking the Okehampton Firing Range boundary, and pick a careful path downhill among the slippery moss-covered rocks. Make a note of the line to Yes Tor, which will soon be invisible; later you will need to cross the river so as to pass close to the southernmost oak trees of Black-a-Tor Copse and then continue on up the opposite slope, crossing a patch of bracken and, further up, a slab of rock on its edge.

The 1240 boundary crosses the West Okement at this scenic point, with Lints Tor beyond.

It takes some time to get through the sloping rockfield and on to more even ground, but, this being Dartmoor, the 'more even' ground is, in fact, a substantial stretch of soft bog draining the hillside into the river below. Consequently, you will now need to make a detour to the south to get around this obstacle. Before you continue down to the valley floor, pause among the old tin-streamings out of the breeze to rest and perhaps have lunch. With the West Okement valley in full view, this is a time and a place to contemplate one's good fortune in being out on Dartmoor on, hopefully, a fine day in spectacular surroundings. On a wet day the whole ambience will, of course, be rather different!

Eventually you will have to face up to a long slog up out of the valley to Yes Tor. But the first obstacle is right next to you, in the form of the West Okement River. Depending on the flow in the river, you may have to go some way downstream before the random arrangement of boulders on its bed enables you to step over to the other side.

In a very short distance, beyond the east bank of the river, the ground begins to rise steeply. In fact, the gradient quickly becomes acute enough to require most people to make frequent stops to catch their breath, allowing another chance to take in the view. Prominent on the opposite hillside are the Slipper Stones, while higher up the valley behind you, the granite boss of Stenga Tor begins to appear on the skyline. Continue upwards by zig-zagging across the slope to reduce the pull on your calf muscles; then, after a long haul, the slope eases and you will find yourself crossing a grassy hillside, with the Black Tor outcrops to your left.

Soon the A30 trunk road comes into view, and further to the west, on the moor itself, you will see the Sourton Tors, along with the terracing of the ice works. On a sunny afternoon a cusp of deep shadow will be filling Corn Hole, below the northern end of Corn Ridge. Above you, meanwhile, the rocky stubs of High Willhays will start appearing on the skyline, and before much longer the short, dry turf of the lower slopes will be giving way to patches of short heather, with intervening wet depressions, on the summit plateau.

Finally, make your weary way over the last few hundred metres to the summit of Yes Tor itself. Having spent much energy on the trials and tribulations of crossing the West Okement valley and climbing the slope, you can now just sit and admire the fantastic view from this high northern bastion of Dartmoor. Southwards, High Willhays is always impressive, especially with the rocks in silhouette against the sun. To the north, the target railway on Black Down is prominent in the middle distance, and beyond this - and all around you for that matter - the scenery is totally mind-blowing.

The view to the south for the 1240 perambulators would have been very much like that of today. But, to the north, the scene would have been very different; the lowlands would probably have been cultivated and grazed to

The summit of Yes Tor, with the military look-out hut.

some degree, but there would, of course, have been few dwellings and farms - how fascinating it would be to see Devon as they saw it then, in the mid-13th century. In terms of their immediate task, the perambulators would now be able to look across the northern moor to their starting point at Cosdon Hill and draw satisfaction from the fact that their duty was almost done.

As for you, you have completed a walk that, because of its arduous nature, you would probably never have contemplated doing other than to retrace the steps of the perambulators. Be warned, this is easily the most tiring section of the 1240 Forest boundary! Soon it will be time to turn wearily away from Yes Tor and set off across Okehampton Common for Meldon Reservoir, the car and the journey home.

──── 12. Yes Tor to Cosdon Hill– 3.9 miles ────

Starting point: New Bridge, on the Black-a-ven Brook.
Grid ref: SX 596 904.
Other important information: Walk lies partly within the Okehampton Firing Range.
Total length of walk: Around 9 miles, assuming you retrace your steps from Cosdon Hill to the western limb of the military loop road and then walk back to New Bridge.

To reach the starting point drive into Okehampton and up the steep road to Okehampton Camp. Beyond the camp, swing to the left through the open barrier (it will be closed and guarded if there is firing planned for that day on the Okehampton Range) and head anti-clockwise along the military loop road. A varied journey over smooth tarmac, loose stones and massive potholes will eventually bring you to New Bridge (below East Mil Tor), where there is a small parking area on the west side of the road.

The half-hour walk from New Bridge across the valley of the Red-a-ven Brook to Yes Tor is direct and straightforward, in contrast to the ascent from the West Okement on the previous leg. Once you have reached the summit, even if you are being buffeted by a stiff breeze, take the opportunity of enjoying the fine view of most of your route to Cosdon. Immediately ahead of you, the walk will take you just south of the rock stack of West Mil Tor and on towards the enclosures of East Okement Farm, beyond which is the Belstone ridge, dwarfed by the massive bulk of Cosdon Hill further to the east.

It is now time to head off on the final 3.9 miles of the perambulation, the first part being an imaginary straight line from Yes Tor to Cullever Steps - 2 miles away on the East Okement. Pick your way down the north-eastern slope of Yes Tor, noting the evidence that this large rock stack was, aeons ago, even larger than it is today, much of it now lying in ruins in an extensive area of clitter. Further down the slope, sacrifice linear exactitude for easier walking and cross the Red-a-ven Brook where three large boulders allow you to step over easily. For a short distance you will be floundering through rather boggy ground, but this soon gives way to firm terrain that continues all the way up to the top of West Mil Tor. Behind you, to the south, the sun will mark in shadow the basin edge of the upper valley of the Red-a-ven Brook.

Pass below the top of West Mil Tor, revert to your straight-line route and make your way down the hill and over the military road to the target railway. This is a fascinating military artefact, the aim of which was to provide practice in shooting at a moving target. A straight section of track, turning loop, points and a shed for storing the target-bearing trucks are all still in place. Nearby is a static target, comprising a massive rusty iron slab mounted on a frame and riddled with gouges from successful strikes from bullets and cannon fire. The military authority's view is that the best way of preserving such fascinating remains is to continue to use them. Certainly, when I visited the site in March 2002, it appeared as though this philosophy was being put into practice, for nearby there were several new sections of iron lying on wooden pallets and awaiting installation to form a new target.

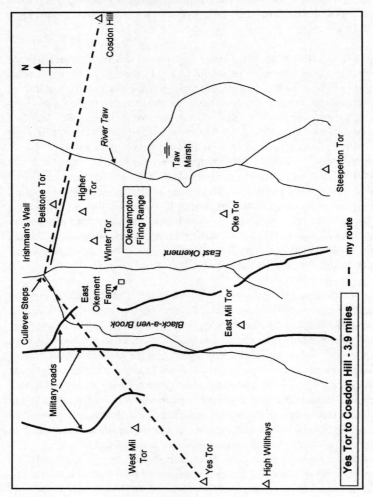

Yes Tor to Cosdon Hill - 3.9 miles

– – my route

The 1240 boundary passes the military target railway, with West Mil Tor in the background.

Carry on over the heath, with Row Tor to your left. There may now be plenty of human activity around you, with walkers and perhaps a few cars using the military road. Cross the western limb of the road and make for the northern end of the East Okement Farm enclosures, even though this means that you are now deviating from the notional straight line to Cullever Steps. Next, jump over the Black-a-ven brook just downstream of a near-natural weir and then proceed gingerly over ground that will quake unnervingly under your feet. Stepping from tussock to tussock, pick your way across to the eastern limb of the loop road, follow it northwards to the bridge over the brook and then turn eastwards down the hill towards the East Okement.

This little valley is sheltered and probably the only effect of any breeze will be to waft a faint smell of cattle from over the enclosure wall of East Okement Farm. To your right, the Black-a-ven Brook tumbles noisily down towards its confluence with the East Okement at Cullever Steps. When I walked this leg of the perambulation the sounds were completed by the muffled drone of a tractor spreading muck on a bright green meadow on East Okement Farm. These simple, timeless sounds and smells of Dartmoor in warm sunshine made my walk all the more memorable.

It is worth diverting from the track to inspect a substantial standing stone over to your right. Next to it is a much smaller stone, but each is engraved with the letters 'OP B', indicating the boundary between Okehampton and

Belstone parishes. Joining this boundary is, of course, that of the Forest itself, and this now reveals itself on the ground. A short way to the east is a straight section of the East Okement Farm enclosure and, beyond it, is Irishman's Wall, its geometrical regularity prominent among the haphazard spread of clitter on the western slope of the Belstone Tors. The boundary stone, the enclosure wall and Irishman's Wall all line up more or less exactly along the line of the Forest boundary as it climbs up over Belstone. Irishman's Wall, incidentally, was a short-lived attempt by reputedly bare-footed Irishmen to enclose part of the commons in the late 18th/early 19th century. It was soon substantially destroyed by the parishioners of Belstone!

Tackling the stiff climb up the Belstone ridge, you should now follow the line of Irishman's Wall as closely as you can over the tumble of clitter. Near the top of the ridge, the wall becomes higher, and its pattern of construction is well shown in places. On the summit itself you pass between two logan stone formations; attempts to rock either stone are futile, as each is firmly supported in at least two places.

The top of the Belstone ridge gives a fine view back over the tranquil setting of East Okement Farm. This was established by the military authorities in 1878 and is known locally as Hartor Farm, after the stump of rock on the nearby hill. Somehow the close-grazed green turf of the enclosed meadows is not out of place beneath the rugged landscape all around it, the ordered layout of the farm complementing its wild surroundings perfectly.

The 1240 boundary crosses the River Taw at this point.

After you have passed over the crown of the ridge follow Irishman's Wall down into the next valley, which is that of the River Taw. Below you, to the right, is the great natural amphitheatre of Taw Marsh, threaded by the lazy meanders of the river and punctuated by patches of water. At its southern end, Taw Marsh is blockaded by the bulk of Steeperton Tor, while to the north the level floor of the valley continues until it dives out of sight into Belstone Cleave.

On reaching the western bank of the Taw, you will notice that hereabouts it is set in a channel that looks to have been artificially deepened in the past for tin streaming. Moreover, you will soon realise that you will be unable to cross it where the notional Forest boundary line does so (about a quarter of a mile downstream of the ford) because the river is wide and certainly clear enough for one to see that it is also very deep! So instead go upstream for about 50 metres and find a point where the channel is narrower and the sides overhang, thus reducing the width still further. Then, if you are fit enough, put anything you are carrying securely into your pockets or rucksack, take a run-up of several feet, jump and...land safely on the other side!

Once you are on the opposite bank of the river, climb away from the Taw and soon you will reach a plateau-like shoulder of Cosdon, a bulky feature that is nonetheless not very prominent unless you actually walk over it. The plateau is known locally as Queenie Meads and gives birth to a stream called Lady Brook, marked wrongly as 'Ivy Tor Water' on the OS map (Ivy Tor

The summit cairn on Cosdon.

91

Water is actually the short, steeply-graded stream that falls into the Taw in Belstone Cleave, near Ivy Tor, more than a mile downstream). As always, when climbing a Dartmoor hill, a glance behind is worthwhile and here you are presented with a fine view of the western slope of the Belstone ridge and also of Irishman's Wall as it drops down towards the Taw.

At the eastern side of the plateau you will find yourself walking over regular, heather-clad undulations, which are the remains of tin workings of old. Then, leaving Queenie Meads below you, set off up the final slope to the top of Cosdon. As you look westwards, the hills rise like massive ocean breakers - first the Belstone/Oke Tor ridge, then East Mil Tor and finally West Mil Tor, High Willhays and Yes Tor. On you go, the gradual curve of Cosdon's top making the final sighting of the summit cairn a much-anticipated event. And suddenly there it is, a simple pile of stones surrounding a modern OS triangulation point and capping one of the great hills of Dartmoor.

This is the end of your personal perambulation of the Forest of Dartmoor. You should congratulate yourself on having completed 43.2 miles of walking over some of the most intriguing, isolated and inspiring terrain on Dartmoor, following in the footsteps of that extraordinary event - the perambulation of 1240.

Bibliography

I have listed below a few books that contain detailed information about the Forest of Dartmoor, either wholly or in part. There are, of course, many others about the more general topic of walking on Dartmoor and about the history of the moor.

Dartmoor Boundary Markers and other markers on and around the moor by Dave Brewer (Halsgrove, 2002).

Echoes of an Ancient Forest by William Crossing (Forest Publishing, 1994).

Dartmoor's Greatest Walk by Bill Ransom (Devon Books, 1987).

A Perambulation of the Ancient and Royal Forest of Dartmoor and the Venville Precincts: Or, a Topographical Survey of Their Antiquities and Scenery by Samuel Rowe (reprint published by Devon Books, 1985).

Dartmoor A New Study edited by Crispin Gill (David & Charles, 1970).

Index

Two other titles available from the publishers by the same author:–

ESCAPE TO DARTMOOR!
(Impressions of walking in the wilderness)
By Michael Hedges. Price £7.95
ISBN: 0 9527297 2 5 (Paperback, 160 pages)
To anyone living in a city, its suburbs, or even the familiar English countryside, the Dartmoor wilderness is a forbidding, alien landscape. Yet the peace and unspoilt nature of this same environment offer a means of escaping, if only briefly, the pressures of living in the modern world. The author describes seventeen walks out to the remotest parts of Dartmoor, relating his experiences and underlining the powerful impressions which this unique landscape make on anyone who explores its depths. The book is illustrated with many photographs.

DARTMOOR CAPTURED!
(More impressions of walking in the wilderness)
By Michael Hedges. Price £7.95
ISBN: 0 9527297 6 8 (Paperback, 160 pages)
As in his first book, *Escape to Dartmoor!*, Michael Hedges sets out to convey his impressions of walking in the remotest parts of the Dartmoor wilderness. Through the pages of *Dartmoor Captured!*, the reader can join the author as he undertakes a bitterly cold walk out to Bleak House over the frozen wastes of north-western Dartmoor during the 1996 rime frost, and many other expeditions. These include a journey through the grandeur of the West Okement Valley to Cranmere Pool, in the northern morass, and the epic route over the moor from Harford to Okehampton, following the traditional drovers' track across the loneliest stretch of high moorland in England.